The
# MIDDLE EAST
# CHALLENGE
## 1980–1985

Edited by Thomas Naff

### MIDDLE EAST
### RESEARCH INSTITUTE
*University of Pennsylvania*
A Conference Publication

SOUTHERN ILLINOIS UNIVERSITY PRESS
Carbondale and Edwardsville

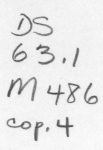

Printed in the United States of America

Designed by Peter Scott and Bob Nance, Design for Publishing

Production Supervised by Richard Neal

**Library of Congress Cataloging in Publication Data**
Main entry under title:

The Middle East challenge, 1980–1985.

"Papers reproduced in this volume are collected
from a workshop . . . sponsored by the Middle East
Research Institute (MERI) of the University of
Pennsylvania in November 1980"—Introd.
   Contents: Introduction / Thomas Naff—Impli-
cations of Middle East leadership / Eric Rouleau—
Response to Eric Rouleau / Michael Sterner—[etc.]
   1. Near East—Politics and government—1945—
Addresses, essays, lectures. I. Naff, Thomas.
II. University of Pennsylvania. Middle East
Research Institute.

DS63.1.M486      320.956      81-5651
ISBN 0-8093-1042-2            AACR2

# Notes on Contributors

GEORGE T. ABED, International Monetary Fund

ODEH ABURDENE, Occidental Petroleum

J. S. BIRKS, World Bank

HERMANN EILTS, Former U.S. Ambassador to Egypt and Saudi Arabia

RAYMOND GARCIA, President, GRC Client Services

WILLIAM G. HYLAND, Center for Strategic International Studies

JOHN V. JAMES, Chairman, President, and CEO, Dresser Industries, Inc.

CHARLES KEELY, Population Council

LAWRENCE R. KLEIN, Professor of Economics, University of Pennsylvania

ROBERT LEGVOLD, Council on Foreign Relations

JOHN H. LICHTBLAU, Executive Director, Petroleum Industry Research Foundation, Inc.

THOMAS NAFF, Director, Middle East Research Institute, University of Pennsylvania

JAMES NOYES, Hoover Institution

WILLIAM B. QUANDT, Brookings Institution

STEPHEN ROSENFELD, *Washington Post*

ERIC ROULEAU, *Le Monde*

C. A. SINCLAIR, World Bank

J. A. SOCKNAT, World Bank

MICHAEL STERNER, Deputy Assistant Secretary of State

# Contents

PART III: Other Determinants: Corporate, Congressional,
                Military    151

# Figures and Tables

## Figures

## Tables

# *Preface*

The papers reproduced in this volume are collected from a workshop on "The Middle East Challenge: 1980–1985," which was sponsored by the Middle East Research Institute (MERI) of the University of Pennsylvania in November 1980.

The workshop was based on the premise that there is, in today's world, scarcely an economic or political facet of America's national interest that is not affected by economic, social, and political events in the Middle East. From this challenge emerged the workshop's objective: to produce a series of five-year projections—based on thorough analysis of empirical data by a broad range of experts with many perspectives—of the most probable developments critical to United States relations with the Middle East. The purpose was to enhance the capability of both government and business to devise effective policies and strategies to promote their Middle East interests.

To focus the proceedings, the analyses revolved around one major issue—the prospect for regional stability—which was examined from two perspectives: (1) the basic political determinants for stability in the Middle East and the prospects for achieving relative stability in the next half decade; (2) how the basic social and economic factors of development goals, energy, population, and technology affect the policies and strategies of the principal actors in the Middle East. These perspectives, in turn, embodied such determining factors as new leadership, the peace process, Soviet policies, energy, development strategies, and labor migration and economic growth. Other issues—the potential for American business in the Middle East, the outlook for congressional actions affecting United States-Middle East business, and the military dimensions of Middle East security—were treated in the plenary sessions.

Received wisdom about the Middle East cautions us to beware prophecy. This, for a region of ancient prophetic tradition, may seem paradoxical. But Middle East specialists know that paradox is as deeply entrenched as prophecy in the area and that the Middle East has historically been rich in both prophecy and paradox. This pattern today embraces both the region and its analysts. Augment the risks, deepen the confusions, and intelligent men and women paradoxically rush to hazard predictions (often thinly disguised wishes) about what will or should happen in the Middle East. The present volume stems from the paradoxical proclivity for prophecy of the best Middle East experts.

Justification for the attempt to model the near future of the Middle East lies in the urgent need to know what is happening and what probably will happen. The admonition to beware prophesying about the region is demonstrably rooted in wisdom (for testimony consult those government and corporate analysts whose heads—and not a few of whose hearts—have been cracked by the paradoxes of the contemporary Middle East). But vital interests override the risk of miscalculation and its consequences. Risk can be considerably lessened by projecting from a well-understood past, an endeavor that is usually rewarded by knowledge and insight. We believe this workshop has produced just such an outcome.

Reflecting the countervailing nature of the political, economic, and social forces at work in the Middle East, the contributors to this volume have been selected from many backgrounds; they apply various modes of observation and analysis and answer to the vested interests of many institutions—academic, corporate, government and international. Above all, they are persons whose experience and knowledge have given them deep insight into the Middle East and its problems, past and present. Whatever the specific point of view, they are all professionals who must be taken seriously.

The insights generated by the workshop provide a basis for making intelligent choices. Among the analyses and projections offered, however, the everlasting Middle East paradoxes remain. How well the authors have tamed these paradoxes, and therefore how much respect we should accord their prophecies, must be decided in 1985.

*Philadelphia*  THOMAS NAFF
*March 1981*

# Introduction

# The Middle East in 1985—
# Through a Murky Crystal

### By Hermann F. Eilts

My mission is to offer some thoughts on what the Middle East might look like in 1985. In venturing to do so, I emphasize at the outset that my crystal ball is cloudy, very cloudy, and seems to be becoming more so with each passing day. More than ever I am reminded of Sam Goldwyn's dictum: "Prophesying," he said, "is a risky business especially for the future!" Still, since I am sure that by 1985 all notes taken today will have been lost or mislaid, and hence I will not be called to account, I will venture some speculation on the subject.

In doing so, I start with two basic assumptions. First, whatever success the United States may have in the next five years in conserving energy, it will continue to be heavily dependent upon Middle Eastern oil. This will, in turn, mean a continued active American interest in the stability and security of the Middle East region, coupled with an effort to maintain friendly relations with as many of the area states as possible. Second, the Soviet Union will continue its concern for, and interest in, the Middle East and will compete with the United States for influence in the area.

Viewed from the perspective of Moscow, the Middle East looks quite different from the profile it presents to the West. Given the Soviet paranoia about presumed external threats, the contiguous Middle East area will continue to be viewed as a potential "soft underbelly," to use Churchill's term for the Balkans, which must be safeguarded through the elimination or neutralization of Western influence in the area and the creation there of governments friendly to the Soviet Union. Additionally, whether or not one accepts the accuracy of CIA estimates that the Soviet Union will by May 1985 have a growing requirement for Persian Gulf oil, it will at some point in the next decade or so begin to encounter difficulties in meeting its own petroleum needs and those of its Comecon satellites. As this begins to happen, it will share in the Western interest in having access to Middle East oil and will actively seek ways and means of achieving this. How it will do so is likely to be a critical question in the decade ahead.

3

In the framework that I have sketched, I propose to look at four pertinent aspects that are bound to affect the Middle East in 1985: first, the United States and Soviet leadership issue; second, what Middle Eastern leadership is likely to look like in 1985; third, three situational problems which I consider to be of significance for the area now and in the future—the Arab/Israeli dilemma, Persian Gulf stability, and the question of a more assertive Islamic component of the Middle East equation; and, finally, some economic matters. Since the time available to me to do all of this is limited, you will appreciate that I can touch only briefly on most of these issues without attempting to develop them at length. Some will, in any case, be studied and projected in our discussions of the next three days.

To begin with, the United States has a new American President, Ronald Reagan. His views on the totality of the Middle East problem are still largely unknown, if indeed they have yet been fully formed. By 1985, his first term will have ended. Judging from the views known to be held by, and the public comments of some of his closest foreign policy advisors, President Reagan's approach to the Middle East will be predicated on a strong concern for the security of Israel. This is understandable, and few Americans would question the correctness of such a view. What remains uncertain, however, is the extent of the president's understanding of other factors associated with Middle Eastern issues. Thus, for example, the United States has strong interests in maintaining friendly relations with Arab states, especially Egypt, Jordan, and oil-rich Saudi Arabia. Some sense of balance will be needed if, by 1985, the existing fragile structure of peace in the Middle East is to be maintained and strengthened. It would be a great mistake if the new American president takes Arab friends for granted (President Sadat, Prince Fahd and the Saudi leadership, King Hussein and others) and shows inadequate sensitivity to their genuine concerns.

In my judgment, a period of education, probably taking a year or so before the new Administration fully understands the complexities of the Middle East issues, will be needed. During that period, I fear, there may be a downward trend in the United States' position in the area. I hope that I am wrong, or that the downward trend will be slight, but the concerns already expressed publicly and privately by various Arab leaders about what they consider to be an imbalance in the President's coterie of advisors indicates their worry on this point.

This said, I have considerable confidence in the basic sense of fairness of the president, not to mention the compelling nature of the broad panoply of American interests in the Middle East, which, it seems to me, will sooner or later bring about a realization that careful balance is needed if American interests in the Middle East are to be effectively managed.

Middle East peace remains an essential objective of American policy. We have come a long way in the past six years, under Republican and Democratic presidents alike, in moving in this direction, electoral campaign rhetoric in each instance notwithstanding. The president will, I suspect, before long find himself in that same narrow valley of limited options to achieve peace in the Middle East that previous presidents have quickly found themselves in when dealing with the area. He, like they, will increasingly come to appreciate that a commitment to the security of Israel need not be incompatible with good relations with the Arabs. Thus, by 1985, I expect an administration that is far more aware of the complexities of the Middle East situation than seems to be the case at present. Whatever downward trend may have taken place in the initial period of the new administration will, I believe, be at least recovered by the end of his term. Regrettably, of course, the year 1984 will mark another presidential election campaign, with all of the stresses that such campaigns create for a balanced Middle East policy. Yet this is a quadrennial problem for those friends and allies who look to the United States and, however much the leaders of the Middle East may deplore it, my experience suggests that they have generally become inured to it.

In the Soviet Union, our leading superpower competitor, it is highly unlikely that Brezhnev will still be in office. A new generation of Soviet leadership, new not necessarily in terms of age but in terms of assuming the responsibility of power, will most certainly be at the Soviet helm. It will be less experienced and, I rather suspect, will be prone to a greater degree of venturesomeness on the international scene than was the case with his predecessors. This will be especially true in areas which it conceives to be of direct interest to the Soviet Union, such as the Middle East. If I am right, we can expect a period of more active Soviet probing for increased influence in the Middle East, a search for exposed or vulnerable areas in which such Soviet influence can be more deeply rooted and effective. The chaotic conditions in Iran, always an area of great interest to the Soviets, suggest that that country may by then, if not before, be ripe for such probing.

In saying this, I do not suggest that such Soviet venturesomeness will necessarily be military in nature. Afghanistan, I suspect, has, for a time at least, provided a salutary lesson for the Soviets. But Soviet political action, including military and economic aid as instruments for potential political gains, will be actively employed.

Thus, by 1985, an American administration, more knowledgeable and balanced than indications suggest are presently the case, will be confronting a new Soviet leadership more active and venturesome than that which exists today—politically—in the Middle East ring.

Let me now turn to the question of Middle Eastern leadership. Which of the present leaders of the Middle East are still likely to be politically effective by 1985? I consider it essential to look at this leadership aspect. Whether one likes it or not, it is the political leaderships of the states of the area with which the United States and the Soviet Union must work. Leaders' personal predilections, their perceived notions of internal and external factors that affect their ability to remain in office, their whims and, yes, even their caprices, will, as in the past, continue to govern most policy decisions in the Middle East. Economic and social factors at home and abroad will admittedly play some role in their thinking, but not to the extent that we in academic, business or think-tank circles may sometimes be inclined to believe. To the extent that they do so, however, it will be in terms of leadership perceptions of local economic and social problems (a highly subjective judgment in each case) rather than in terms of objective analysis of economic or social data.

Thus, a Sadat, despite all of the sound economic advice of the IMF, the United States, and others on the need for price stabilization in Egypt, and despite dire predictions of the consequences of failure to tackle this problem now, will continue to be governed by his estimate of the domestic political costs and risks of imposing added food costs upon his people. Similarly, a Qaddafi will continue to conduct his policies on the basis of his ingrained anti-Israeli views and an Assad will do so on the basis of Alawite interests and Syrian Ba'ath party ideology. One could continue with this list ad infinitum. I repeat—it is with the leaders of the Middle East, and not with our perceptions of economic and social trends, that the United States and the Soviets will have to work in the future, as is now the case.

In Israel, Prime Minister Begin will almost certainly be gone as a politically effective leader. By the end of next year, if not before, a Labor government is likely to be in office in that country and will still be in power by 1985. Whether it will be headed by Shimon Peres, as now seems likely, or Yitzhak Rabin, his competitor for power in the Labor party, or by a new generation of Labor leaders, is hard to say. However, it really makes little difference. The Labor party position on the West Bank and Gaza, as articulated by Peres, Rabin and their colleagues, offers at least slightly greater scope for genuine negotiation than does the Likud coalition's autonomy concept. I do not wish to overstate this point, but it clearly offers greater scope than is the case with present West Bank/Gaza autonomy talks.

In Egypt, President Sadat is now sixty-one and by 1985 will be sixty-six. His presidential term ends in 1982, but, as a result of recent legislation, he may remain in office indefinitely. Whether or not President Sadat will still be politically effective in Egypt by 1985 is impossible to predict. Much depends upon him and whatever achievements on progress toward peace in the Middle East have taken place in the past seven years is largely due to his courageous vision. His health is good, so there is a reasonable chance, God willing, that he will still be able to bear the burdens of leadership.

By then, if the Egyptian/Israeli peace treaty is fulfilled in accordance with its provisions, Egypt will have recovered the Sinai (in April, 1982) and normalization of relations between Egypt and Israel will have had a five year run. However, as I have frequently contended, the quality of the incipient relationship will depend in large measure upon meaningful progress or otherwise in West Bank/Gaza autonomy talks. If there is no meaningful progress on the Palestinian question by then, we should expect signs of faltering in the new Egyptian/Israeli relationship. I do not expect that the peace treaty will be broken, but there will be increasing complaints of each against the other. These will sour what has been achieved and make difficult increased achievement in bilateral relations.

Incidentally, by 1985 I would also expect some downward trend in United States/Egyptian relations, brought about by Egyptian dissatisfaction with perceived limitations on American military and economic aid.

President Sadat's successor is likely to be Vice President Husni Mubarak. Like Sadat, Mubarak believes in the peace process. He is a fine person, but—understandably—lacks the president's long experience, immense reservoir of patience and farsighted strategic vision. He will in time gain these, and President Sadat is giving him increased executive authority, but one cannot compress into five short years the comprehensive lessons of a lifetime such as Sadat has led. So long as Sadat remains in office, and I hope it will be a long time, I believe that he will have the patience to continue the peace process, despite the obvious obstacles and despite criticism from Arabs and some of the Egyptian intelligentsia. Under Sadat, internal differences within Egypt do exist, but they are minimized. It may not be so easy for a successor who, in the very nature of things, is more likely to be challenged at home and to feel it necessary to resort to authoritarian measures to cope with such challenges.

In Saudi Arabia, King Khalid has for many years suffered from cardiac ailments. He has had to pace himself in terms of his activities and he has never felt comfortable with the onerous duties of government. Since the death of King Faisal in 1975, Crown Prince Fahd has been executive agent for the management of Saudi governmental matters. He is fifty-nine and, God willing, should still be in charge by 1985. Prince Fahd has been important to the United States. While not agreeing with the Carter Administration's management of the peace process, including Camp David and the Egyptian/Israeli peace treaty, he has retained a measure of confidence in President Carter's desire to arrive at a just and durable peace. Because of this, he has continued to work with the United States on such essential matters as maintaining high petroleum production levels. Some of his brothers, nephews, and other Saudi leaders are less enamored of their American connection. Many do not believe that they have gotten a fair return in terms of American efforts to achieve a fair Arab/Israeli settlement for their cooperation on oil matters.

Fahd, like the rest of the Saudi leadership, will be watching closely the stances adopted by the Reagan administration in the next four years on Arab/Israeli peace issues. Fahd values his American connection, but it would be a mistake for any American administration to assume that this is solely dependent upon some sort of a vague United States security commitment to Saudi Arabia. Resolution of the Palestinian issue in some fashion at least passably acceptable to the Palestinians and Arabs at large is, I know, a high priority concern of Prince Fahd. The nature of the United States/Saudi relationship in 1985 will depend in large measure not only upon a security situation in the Persian Gulf, but also upon vigorous action by the Reagan administration to move toward an Arab/Israeli peace, including a resolution of the Palestinian problem. It would be a grave mistake for the Reagan administration to take Saudi Arabia for granted, as has all too often been done by previous administrations. Fahd is a strong leader, one who wants to work with the United States, but American inaction on the Middle East peace process or total partiality toward Israel is certain to undermine his own ability at home to maintain the closeness of that association.

In Libya, Qadaffi is now only forty-three. Barring unforeseen circumstances, he will most likely still be around in 1985 and will continue to be a thorn in the American side. His resources, including petrodollars, will continue to be enormous. As in the past, he will continue to use them capriciously or otherwise against the United States and against Arab leaders friendly to the Unites States.

Though this will be unhelpful, one hopeful note can be sounded. I recall being present many years ago at a Baghdad Pact meeting at which a British Foreign Secretary urged the late Prime Minister of Iraq, Nuri Sa'id Pasha, to use more Iraqi money to win Syrian, Jordanian, and Lebanese support for the Pact. Nuri, in his typically pungent fashion, demurred. He commented, "Mr. Secretary, let me tell you from my many years of experience with Arabs one basic fact of life: you can never buy an Arab, you can only rent him." Nuri Pasha was not trying to be funny. There was a good deal of profundity in his observation. What he was in effect saying was that the use of money, as an instrument of policy, was even then limited in time and space. It had no permanent effect. This is even more true today. Inflation has eroded the value of money as an instrument of policy. It now costs more to try to buy support and the time frame for such support rentals is sharply reduced. Thus, while Qaddafi's disruptive actions will remain a threat, I submit that they will not be unmanageable in scope.

In Syria, President Hafiz al-Assad is encountering increasing domestic difficulties. For the moment, through suppressive action at home and sabre rattling with his neighbors, he seems to be holding out. Yet it is difficult to believe that Hafiz al-Assad will still be in charge in 1985. His successor may be his brother, Rifa'at al-Assad, who from an American— and from a Syrian—point of view would be worse than Hafiz. However, Rifa'at al-Assad, despite the military assets at his disposal, is hardly likely to be a strong successor. Given widespread Syrian disaffection with the rule of the Alawite minority, and dissensions within that minority, a Sunni military successor strikes me as a more likely possibility. The change, I suspect, will be brought about by violent means. The Muslim Brotherhood in Syria, while perhaps temporarily suppressed, will increasingly have to be taken into account by the Syrian leadership. Whichever is the case, I fear that the Syrian role in the Middle East peace process will remain unconstructive. The one exception might be if Israel were willing to give up all or part of the Golan Heights in return for normalization of Syrian/Israeli relations, but this hardly seems in the cards.

The Palestinian leadership, also an essential element in the peace process, may well change in the next five years. Yassir Arafat, though not an old man, is not physically well. By 1985, there is likely to be a shift in the top echelons of the PLO. The extent of that shift, whenever it takes place, will depend in large measure on whether or not the Reagan Administration can persuade the Palestinian community at large that it is seeking a just settlement for the Palestinian problem.

As one who has been involved in the peace process for a long time, I keep hoping that a Palestinian leadership will emerge which will be willing to take a chance on participating in a rational peace process. I confess, however, that I see few prospects for such an attitudinal change by the date that we are discussing. If anything, the political shift of PLO leadership is more likely to drift toward the left. An American dialogue with the

PLO, if conducted under proper conditions, could help to arrest such a drift, and there is perhaps a slight chance that this will come about in the next five years. So long as the PLO conglomerate remains as fragmented as it is, and remains under Syrian dominance, and Israeli positions toward the Palestinians remain as adamant as they are, consensus will continue to dictate Palestinian—read PLO—views. This means lowest common denominator reactions, equatable with negativism, at a time when strong and united leadership is necessary if the Palestinians are to play a constructive part in the peace process. Conceivably, of course, Arafat may mellow a bit with age, but this will only lead to greater challenges to his role.

In Iran, the Ayatollah Khomeini, as Eric Rouleau reminded some of us the other evening and may repeat in this session, may be with us for longer than we think. Yet, by 1985, the actuarial tables should surely be against him. His demise, whenever it comes, will create serious turmoil in Iran. Between whenever that happens and 1985, forces of the left and right in Iran will be engaged in a bitter struggle for control. It is doubtful that Khomeinis putative successor, Ayatollah Muntazori, or any other Iranian religious leader, even operating in the context of the all-important *Faghih* role stipulated in the new Iranian constitution, can have the balancing influence on internal Iranian politics that Khomeini has managed to exercise. By 1985, after a likely period of bloodshed within Iran, I would expect an Iranian government still retaining a strong Shi'i flavor, but with a greater seasoning of secular Iranian nationalism.

Relations between the United States and Iran, in my view, will never return to what they were under the Shah. Indeed, we should not strive for such a relationship, which was built on sand. The hostage issue is behind us—in the sense that the hostages have been released. Conceivably, by 1985, a new United States/Iranian relationship can begin to be forged, based upon mutual respect for each other's interests, upon some more direct dialogue, and upon some kind of cooperation to assure the security of the Persian Gulf. The Soviet threat to Iran exists and could offer a basis for an element of cooperation between our two countries without the imputation of American interference in Iranian affairs. Iranians are paranoic, however, and the development of a new relationship between our two countries will take time and patience. Frustrations will strew its path. Yet, in my judgment, it is a reasonable possibility and should be an objective of American foreign policy in the new administration.

I neglected to speak of Jordan. King Hussein is still likely to be an active political figure in 1985, but will remain in the same difficult position that he is in now. In my judgment, he is in a psychological position to join in the Middle East peace process, even if his geographical position, wedged between Syria and Iraq and with an ever-present Palestinian encumbrance, limits his maneuverability. Conceivably, his improved relations with Iraq in the wake of the Iraqi/Iranian conflict may give him an element of greater leeway to participate in peace negotiations. It would be a mistake, however, to assume that King Hussain can be persuaded in 1985, any more than now, to negotiate giving up most of the West Bank to Israel or give up the Arab/Muslim claim to Jerusalem. For political reasons, he cannot do that; for personal psychological reasons, he will not do so.

I have sought to cover the principal leaders of the area. Obviously, in speaking of the Middle East, there are others in North Africa, Turkey and elsewhere. Time constraints make it impossible to discuss these peripheral leaders—peripheral not in the sense of unimportance, but in terms of being less relevant to the major Middle East issues we will continue to face in the coming decade. I have consciously sought to focus on likely leaders and states which affect our primary situational problems.

Let me now turn briefly to these problems.

First and foremost, of course, is the Arab/Israeli conflict. For the past two years, American policy has operated on the basis of the Camp David accords of 1978. In this framework, an Egyptian/Israeli peace has been successfully brokered. I know from personal experience how much effort and agony on the part of the American, Israeli, and Egyptian leaderships went into forging the Camp David accords. For Israel and for Egypt, Camp David was a seminal achievement, especially in terms of creating a new relationship of peace between these two states.

Yet the price paid vis-a-vis Palestinian aspirations was high. For the past year and a half, periodic public claims on the American side notwithstanding, there has been no meaningful progress on Palestinian autonomy. The hoped-for dialectic of compromise between Israeli and Egyptian views on West Bank/Gaza self-government has failed to materialize. Egyptian leadership in the Arab world, a prominent factor in the American decision to begin the peace process with Egypt, has disappeared—at least for the time being. Egypt is isolated in the Arab and Islamic worlds. The United States is accused of colluding with Israel to achieve the latter's long held objective of separating Egypt from the Arab world. Our European allies and many others openly decry Camp David as dead. Why not then bury Camp David once and for all?

While I am a critic of some aspects of Camp David, I would emphasize that this cannot easily be done. A major American objective should be to preserve what Camp David has achieved in terms of an Egyptian/Israeli settlement. This should not be taken for granted; it needs deeper rooting before it can grow and flourish. At the same time, Camp David is not the answer to the overall Middle East peace process.

The time has come, it seems to me, when we must search for another way, another forum, to permit broader participation in the Middle East peace process. The straightjacket of West Bank/Gaza autonomy, as envisaged in the vague language of the Camp David "General Framework" document, is inadequate and demonstrably unacceptable in the Arab world. The Camp David process must graduate into something broader, in terms of area participation and outside guarantors, if there is to be continued progress for peace in the Middle East. Camp David has fulfilled its purpose, not perhaps to the extent that President Carter had hoped, but still significantly. The "Camp David" imprimatur should now be discarded in favor of something more acceptable in the Middle East as a whole.

I have no easy solutions to the problem of an Arab/Israeli peace. There are none, and I certainly expect no solution by 1985. The important question, I submit, is whether by 1985 we will have moved forward in the direction of a solution or backwards. This will depend in part, but only in part, upon the new American administration of President Reagan.

As I suggested earlier, I envisage a slight downward trend in the first year or so of that administration as it learns the ropes and the facts, and realizes the need for balance. It will do this, in my judgment. American interests in the area demand it. I expect, therefore, that by 1985 there will be a perceptible, even if slow, improvement in Arab/Israeli negotiations. I believe the will is there on the part of President Reagan; his options, as I suggested before, are likely to be limited; his administration's efforts to grapple with the problem, while perhaps initially fumbling, will steadily assume a greater sense of sureness. More than anything else, the Reagan administration will have to create not only in Israel, but also in the Arab and European worlds, a sense of confidence in its desire to conduct a fair and balanced policy between conflicting views.

I wish I could be more definite on this critical element, but solutions to its component elements will not fall into place quickly. Legitimate Palestinian rights, whatever that may mean, will have to become a part of the Reagan administration's foreign policy vocabulary if by 1985 United States interests in the Arab world are to be preserved and expanded.

Next let me turn to the Persian Gulf. The current Iraqi/Iranian war is but part of a series of problems besetting that critical area—described by President Carter as a "vital" American interest, one which the United States would fight to preserve against foreign (read Soviet) threats. Whether the putative Soviet threat to the Gulf is as clear and imminent as the Carter Doctrine implies is subject to debate. I, for one, believe the threat to American interests in the Gulf stems more from unresolved political issues than it does from Soviet military designs, but United States concern for the Gulf area is understandable and justified.

Regardless of which side wins the Iraqi/Iranian war—if indeed there is a clearcut winner, which I rather doubt—we will be left with a sore that will most certainly fester. Conceivably, some—even if not all—Iraqi territorial objectives will be met, though neither side will topple the governmental structure of the other. Some kind of a truce, not a real peace, will ultimately develop, but it will merely buy time before the next round of overt or covert manifestation of bitterness and enmity of one toward the other. If either side should decisively prevail in the present conflict (a not very likely occurrence in my view), its preeminence in the Gulf area will create new tensions or even pose threats for governments friendly toward the United States.

By 1985, however, tensions in the Gulf area will most likely be acute—tensions arising not only from Iraqi/Iranian animosity (a hardy perennial), but also from internal unrest in the Gulf states themselves. A protracted Iraqi/Iranian stalemate, which I admit would carry with it the risk of spillover into other areas of the Gulf, could defang the effectiveness of both Iraqi and Iranian ill-wishers of the United States, at least for a time, and reduce their capacity for mischief-making.

Even if this happens, however, social unrest in the Gulf states will grow. The quest for greater responsibility in the affairs of government, which already characterizes the aspirations of the growing body of American- and Western-trained bureaucrats and technocrats in the Gulf states, will intensify in the years ahead. Thus far, it has been possible to purchase acquiescence in peripheral roles by paying high salaries and offering perquisites in place of responsibility. By 1985 this palliative will be increasingly wearing thin. The United States, if it is not careful, will find itself the scapegoat—à la Iran—in seeming to be preventing this through active support of family governmental structures. It is ironic, and yet perhaps understandable in our current campus atmospheres, that so many young Arabs (and others) trained in American universities emerge sharply critical of United States policies toward the Middle East.

It is, of course, not only the technocrats trained in American universities whose restiveness will increase in the years ahead. Military officers in Gulf states are, and will be, similarly affected. With few exceptions, Middle East military establishments are notoriously unprofessional. Yet the officer corps have at their disposal a physical potential for asserting stronger influence on the governments which they presumably serve. What has been lacking since pre-1967 Nasser is a charismatic leader and an ideology in the cause of which they may seek to assert themselves. Thus far, neither Qaddafi nor the Ba'ath enjoys sufficient area-wide prestige to enlist ideological support from officer corps in the Gulf region. A mixture of close governmental scrutiny and timely removal of suspected disaffected elements, coupled with the positive elements of pay, perquisites, and modern-equipment incentives, has enabled governmental leaders to manage the military. Perhaps this will still be so in 1985, perhaps not. The potential threat from this sector of society is omnipresent and will at the very least probably be more finely honed by mid-decade.

Added to these potentially disruptive factors is the expatriate problem. Throughout the Arab states of the Gulf, Iraq excepted, there are sizeable unassimilated expatriate communities, in some cases outnumbering the indigenous populations. The diverse nature of these expatriate communities—Palestinian, Iranian, Pakistani, Baluchi, Korean, Japanese, Western—has a certain "checks and balances" effect in any given state. Those who are more politically minded, however, such as the Palestinians and Iranians, are discontented and constitute a potentially destabilizing force in individual Gulf states. Unresolved problems, such as the Arab/Israeli issue and the Iraqi/Iranian war, simply exacerbate this threat. There is no sure way to estimate how serious the expatriate threat will be in the Gulf by 1985, but it is a festering sore that cannot be ignored and will be more serious by 1985. Economic bandaid approaches to controlling it by then may no longer suffice.

I want now to turn to the somewhat more amorphous, but always present, subject of Islam as it will affect the Middle East in the decade ahead. Americans, as a nation of discoverers, have in the past year and a half "discovered" Islam. Today, most Americans, including many in government, tend to see Islam through the prism of Khomaini and Islamic militancy and to view it as inherently negative and hostile. This is a distorted image and one that obscures the fundamental psychological problems that Muslim communities everywhere are facing.

Military Islamic resurgences, in my experience, are cyclical in nature. Yet ferment, questioning, frustration is ever-present in Islamic societies. Today, Khomaini's Iranian Islamic revolution epitomizes, among other things, militant Muslim protest over Islam's perceived low state in the world. Twenty years ago, also in violent form, it was Hassan al-Banna and the Ikhwan al-Muslimin (the Muslim Brotherhood) in Egypt. A generation from now or earlier, even after the effects of Khomaini have abated, these will doubtless be a new manifestation of Islamic resurgence, motivated by frustration over real or perceived foreign domination.

Yet this type of militant surge of Muslim restiveness, I submit, reflects the more fundamental challenge that Islamic communities have long sought to grapple with, namely the challenge of modernization. Modernization, all too often equated with Westernization and therefore decried by many Muslims as antagonistic to Islamic values, is an ongoing concern in Muslim communities. I have met few Muslims in the past thirty-five years who have rejected the concept of some sort of modernization or the need for it. The question with which they have wrestled has been how to adjust their societies to the introduction of *selected* accoutrements of modernity, usually drawn from the West, without undermining fundamental values in the process. It is easy to pose the question, yet so difficult to find meaningful answers to it. The *salafiya* movement in Islamic society, the originator of which was the great Egyptian reformer of the turn of the century, Muhammed Abduh, but which has over the past eighty years regressed in its reformist thrust, is still actively seeking to confront the modernization issue. Is the Islamic community not capable, it asks, of creating its own physical instruments of selective modernization, without aping Western patterns, for the greater good of its members and without perverting their values? Apart from fervent belief that it is capable of doing so, it has, thus far, been short on specifics. The quest, nevertheless, goes on. Khomaini eventually will go, but we should bear in mind that this more fundamental restiveness in a large part of the global Muslim community is a more or less permanent factor, latent at some times, active at others, which we in the West should bear in mind. Some dialectical accommodation needs to be sought.

A great deal more needs to be said on Islam in the contemporary world, but my time is running out and I still want to comment briefly on two economic issues that will, I believe, characterize the Middle East in the coming decade.

I am convinced that by 1990 we are going to see a sharp reduction in the oil production of most of the Gulf countries, Saudi Arabia included, for reasons of conservation. There is a growing groundswell of informed public opinion in the oil-producing states that present high production levels are detrimental to the future well-being of the peoples in those states. Why should they undertake such sizeable oil output when the petrodollars it produces rapidly erode in terms of purchasing power, are unneeded for development purposes, and serve only to strengthen United States and Western economies? A barrel of oil left in the ground now, it is argued, is of greater value than the dollar value it would receive today. So why go on producing at present levels? Reductions, yes sizeable reductions in production, are needed to protect the longer range interests of the peoples of the area.

Those who control this are in some cases politically motivated, imbued with a sense of dissatisfaction or even bitterness about perceived United States' insensitivity to Arab concerns. In many instances, however, there is no such capricious motivation or at least it does not predominate. Genuine economic compulsions motivate many Arab conservationists. Nor is there any desire deliberately to cripple Western economies. There simply is a feeling that full value in the broadest sense is not being received for excess production and that the interests of future generations of Saudis, Kuwaitis and others are being mortgaged by present high levels of oil production.

If Saudi Arabia has for the past year produced 9.5 mbd, this is due largely to Prince Fahd. He is criticized by some of his own family, not to mention other Saudi leaders, for maintaining production at this level when Saudi Arabia does not need the income and is perceived to be ignored as far as its concerns about the Arab/Israeli issue are concerned. American security protection for Saudi Arabia, such as it is, is hardly a compelling justification to continue excessive production levels in order to please the United States.

By 1985, I would expect pressures on Fahd from conservationists—politically or economically motivated—to have intensified to a point where it becomes increasingly difficult, in the absence of demonstrable progress toward real peace in the Middle East, for the Saudi leadership to ignore or override it. Farther down the road, after Prince Fahd, such domestic pressures will become even more potent.

In the meantime, Arab investments in the United States will remain high despite worries over the precedent set by the freezing of Iranian assets. As the European investment market increases, however, as it will, there will be a greater Arab tendency to diversify their foreign investments. There will be less new Arab investment in the United States.

As far as American business is concerned, United States antiboycott and tax legislation has already seriously hurt American firms who wish to compete with European and Japanese firms in the Middle East. By 1985, unless corrected in the next year or so, the task of recovering such commercial opportunity losses will be increasingly difficult. I wish I could be encouraged on this score, but I frankly see no meaningful relief in sight for American firms. In that blithe fashion, which sometimes characterizes politically motivated congressional actions, we will have effectively hamstrung many American firms who wish to engage in business in the Middle East.

More will be said about all of these subjects in the course of the conference proceedings. Hence, since it is already late, I shall conclude my oral and perforce hasty ramble through the mists of speculation of what the Middle East might look like five years hence.

Of one thing we may be certain: it will still be there, it will still be difficult and, alas, most of its problems will still be distinctly recognizable for those of us who grapple with them today.

Thank you.

# Part I:
# Political Determinants of Stability

# Prospects for Instability and New Leadership

## By Eric Rouleau

THE FIRST CHALLENGE posed by the Middle East is its unpredictable character. If a meeting similar to our present one had been held exactly ten years ago with the same theme on its agenda, how many experts would have contended that, during the coming decade, the region would be one of the most stable in the world? At that time, everything seemed to indicate that the area would be passing through a stormy period: in November 1970, General Asad took power in Syria while King Hussein saved his throne after fierce strife between the Jordanian army and Palestinian freedom fighters; a year earlier, the Sanoussi dynasty had been toppled by Colonel Qadhafi's coup d'etat; several months before, a nationalist and pro-Communist military junta had gained control of the Sudan; in 1967, a leftist guerilla movement had driven Great Britain out of strategically important South Yemen and several Arab states had been severely shaken by the cataclysm of the June 1967 debacle.

Let us establish from the outset that, contrary to what could have been predicted legitimately, the decade of the 1970s was, in a global sense, one of unexpected political continuity. With the exception of Iran, not a single Middle Eastern regime was toppled by violence, nor did any undergo fundamental transformation. Furthermore, this was true despite important socio-economic changes (in the oil producing countries in particular), despite an all-pervasive atmosphere of tension, despite ethnic conflicts (for example between the Arabs and the Kurds of Iraq), and most important, despite several wars (Jordanian-Palestinian in 1970, Lebanese-Palestinian in 1975–1976, and, of course, Arab-Israeli in October 1973).

However, this stability does not necessarily signify harmonious evolution. Almost all of the regimes in the Middle East experienced serious crises which could have been fatal to them. Examples are the coup d'etat in the Sudan in July 1971 that almost brought to power a pro-Communist group; the Palestinian commando attempt to assassinate King Hussein and members of his government in the beginning of 1973; the popular upheaval in Egypt in January 1977; and the occupation of the Great Mosque

21

in Mecca by several hundred rebels in November 1979. Most of the countries of the region experienced plots of one kind or another which were foiled, discreetly or otherwise.

Thus, one realizes that this "stability"—not really an appropriate term to designate the political immobilism in most Middle Eastern countries—was largely superficial. It was maintained by factors, varying from one country to another, which had as their common denominator strict police vigilance. With only a few exceptions, strong and ruthless security forces repressed all forms of protest, even those of an ideological order. While the repression was more or less subtle in some countries, it was bloody in others; summary executions, assassinations, and massacre contributed to the maintenance of some regimes which otherwise would probably have disappeared during the past decade.

Paradoxically, it would seem that the monarchies and princedoms in the Middle East are built on more solid foundations today than are the republics. This phenomenon is true for several reasons. The legitimacy of the ruling families—based on history, religion, and strong tribal ties—is, quite naturally, greater than that of political parties or of men who imposed themselves more recently and usually by military force. In one sense, King Hussein today enjoys a more solid popular base in Jordan than does General Asad in Syria, and the Emir of Kuwait enjoys greater authority among his people than do the leaders in the Yemen Arab Republic (North Yemen). On a more general level, oil-producing countries have naturally greater means than do others to satisfy the needs of their populations and thereby, to silence existing or potential opposition. The massive revenues available (especially since the large oil price increases of 1973–74) have allowed them to spread even more widely the social benefits of the "welfare state," and, above all, to distribute part of the oil "manna" to an intermediate layer of the population, the interests of which coincided, up to a certain point, with those of the oligarchies in power. Furthermore, relative social calm is assured by the large-scale use of foreign labor: the nonnatives who leave their homelands in search of jobs which enable them to send money back are less tempted to engage in "subversive" activities when they know they risk expulsion. In this way, labor conflicts are "resolved" even before they occur and it was only rarely in the past decade that the authorities needed to resort to violence in this sphere: for example the intervention by Saudi security forces in the oilfield of the Eastern Province in November 1979 was inevitable because they had to repress demonstrations staged by natives of the Shi'i sect.

Although more limited financially, the leaders of the nonoil producing countries were able to assure a semblance of stability by being flexible; some of them showed a surprising ability to adapt. For example, despite his military victory of 1970–71, King Hussein wisely worked out a *modus vivendi* with the PLO without, however, agreeing to any fundamental concessions. In this way, he was able to reestablish good relations with that half of his subjects which is of Palestinian origin and with the population of the West Bank, which Israel occupied during the June 1967 war. This two-fold success facilitated Jordan's return to the Arab fold from which it had been excluded after the bloody confrontation with the *fedayin* in September 1970.

The Ba'athist regimes in Syria and Iraq consolidated their foundations during the first few years of the decade while following parallel and, in some respects, similar political paths. General Asad in Damascus, like Saddam Hussein in Baghdad, acquired a greater degree of legitimacy by securing the cooperation of several political parties or factions in a "National Progressive Front"—an advisory body which in no way weakened the "leadership role" (in actuality, hegemony) of the Ba'ath party. Taking a course opposite to that of his leftist predecessors, the Syrian president was, in the beginning, able to win the sympathy, or at least the favorable neutrality, of the "bazaaris" (the influential merchant class) by liberalizing somewhat certain sectors of the economy. Both General Asad and Saddam Hussein facilitated the enrichment of a "new bourgeoisie," as President Sadat did in Egypt. However, unlike him, they abstained from presenting their economic policy as an "infitah" (opening up) toward capitalists and, therefore, both in Syria and in Iraq "Arab socialism," or at least its rhetoric, was not watered down by "la raison d'Etat."

As for President Sadat, he was in a much better position than were his Syrian and Iraqi counterparts to engage in a radical revision of "scientific socialism," as well as in a revision of other concepts in the domestic and foreign policies implemented by his predecessor. Nasser had died, leaving behind him a defeated nation, an economy on the edge of bankruptcy, and a people aspiring to social well-being and peace. Sadat found himself in a position to offer, without too much poltical risk, a new path of relative liberalism, the benefits of which could be reaped by trading in the sword of war for the tools of economic progress. His vision was accurate, at least for the middle term, if we are to judge by the favorable reception of the Camp David accords by the Egyptian population.

This enumeration of the principal factors contributing to stability in the Middle East in the 1970s would be incomplete without mention of the role played by foreign powers in the region. Would the survival of the Syrian and Saudi regimes have been secured without the multifaceted aid supplied respectively by the USSR and the U.S. to these two countries? Would order have prevailed in the Emirates of the Persian Gulf if the Shah of Iran had not exercised the role of "policeman" with which he had been invested, or if the U.S. fleet had not cruised off the coast of Oman? Would Sultan Qabus still be on his throne in Muscat today if Iranian troops and British officers had not helped him to defeat Aden-backed guerillas? Is it possible that the Marxist regime of the Yemen Democratic Republic (South Yemen) could have survived for very long without the military, economic, and technological assistance of the USSR, East Germany and Cuba? Of course, the foreign powers are not omnipotent, and their influence, no matter how widespread, is not (nor should it be) always decisive—as American impotence in the face of the Iranian revolution is eloquent proof. Nevertheless, the weight of the superpowers in the balance between forces in the Middle East has shown itself in the last few years to be a determining factor in more than one instance. That is why it would be presumptuous to engage in a serious study of the future of this region without determining its financial, economic and military importance to the global strategies of both the USSR and the U.S.

---

Just as every coin has two sides, the elements of stability in the Middle East carry within them the seeds of instability. The actions of foreign powers are not like a one-way street: while they no doubt contribute to the consolidation of "client states," they also tend to weaken "enemy" regimes. The revival of the cold war, the exclusion of the USSR from the peace process in the Middle East, the Iranian revolution, and the Red Army occupation of Afghanistan will all no doubt contribute to an intensification of East-West rivalry and frictions in the Middle East. For example, were the Tehran regime to draw closer to Moscow, an offensive against all of the region's conservative or "pro-American" countries could be expected and the confrontation that would follow could provoke an upheaval, the characteristics and extent of which are impossible to determine in the present circumstances.

If foreign interventions have a "speed-up" effect, internal factors which generate the dynamics of change ripen slowly but unavoidably. In this respect, the oil-producing countries are more exposed because they are rich. While their policies of massive investment enrich the "happy few," they also bring about the disintegration of traditional society, usually tribal in structure, and socio-economic change comes with brutal speed. Sedentarized nomads and uprooted peasants, sucked up by the oil fields and the industrial complexes, suffer psychological and cultural traumas that eventually lead to political alienation. The rupturing of ties with a tribal or agrarian environment and with ancestral mores and customs, leads, quite naturally, to a questioning of structures based on traditional allegiances. Demographic concentrations and the constraints of urban life do not lend themselves to the type of personal relationship that sheiks, princes, and even kings had with their proteges in the past. The institution of the *majlis*, a democratic forum for exchanges between the governing and the governed in the countries of the Arabian peninsula, is today often not much more than a formality.

The "welfare state" which is on one hand a kind of appeasement, simultaneously generates factors of conflict. Satisfying the elementary needs of the population (with jobs, food, lodging, health care, and education) paradoxically increases its level of expectation to a degree proportionate to the gap which money has created between its upper and lower strata. It may be added here that it has been observed world-wide that social discontent is caused not so much by legitimate claims but rather by differences in the living standards of members of the same community. The frustrations under these circumstances are exacerbated when there is conviction that such inequality is unjustified and that those people who are best provided for, take advantage of social position, of privileges, and of illicit sources of enrichment such as favoritism, nepotism, and corruption.

Under such conditions, religion gradually ceases to be either a source of comfort or the cement that holds together the structures of a theocratic state. The people have increasing difficulty in identifying with leaders who use Islam to perpetuate social injustice, especially if they suspect such leaders of not respecting the Islamic ethic which is imposed on the rest of the population.

The middle classes created by the oil boom are, in this way, just as sensitive to socio-economic change as the lower strata of the population. Entrepreneurs, importers, merchants, bureaucrats, or members of the liberal professions, whether or not they have been educated abroad, are more open to the outside world and, therefore, it is with a much greater degree of difficulty that they accept the constraints of Islamic morality. For example, tens of thousands of women with university qualifications aspire to enter the labor market and to benefit from complete equality with men, in addition to which the process of development makes them indispensable to the proper functioning of an economy, especially that of a country which has serious manpower deficiencies.

Members of the middle classes often have an ambiguous attitude toward the regimes which favor their social mobility. They are at one and the same time favorable and hostile to the established order. Industrial-

ists, businessmen, and merchants in particular would like to see a liberal-
ization of lifestyle and a modern, constitutional system of government
which would make it possible for them to gain access to the political
power system and thereby derive a sense of security now denied them by
the arbitrary character of a hereditary monarchy or a military dictatorship. Their nationalist sentiments are in proportion to the degree of foreign economic penetration they perceive to exist. As the events in Iran
have shown, the middle classes (which are reformist by nature) can fall
into the revolutionary camp in times of crisis when they believe that the
regime to which they have so far given their support is incapable of re-
generating itself.

Police repression is not able to contain popular discontent indefinitely,
nor can it suppress the changes which result from the process of development and which naturally undermine the foundations of a traditional society. In the long run, terror engenders first of all a period of inurement,
followed by defiance on the part of those who must endure it. The turmoil
witnessed recently in such countries as Egypt, Iraq, Syria, Saudi Arabia,
Kuwait, and Bahrain is no doubt a sign of a malaise being felt by most of
the regimes in the Middle East. On the other hand, although it is possible to observe clearly the dynamics of change, it is not easy to define ac-
curately the character of the new groups which eventually might take
over the reins of power.

Since the end of the second World War, three ideologies have served,
in varying degrees, to mobilize the peoples of the Middle East: secular
nationalism, Marxism, and Islam. In order to determine the impact that
these ideologies might have in the coming years, it is not inappropriate to
analyze briefly the influence they have today.

I. *Secular Nationalism.* The wave of nationalism began to break over
the Middle East just after the end of World War II. The defeat of the Axis
powers, the winds of freedom that had begun to blow all over the world,
the promises made to dependent peoples during the war in order to gain
their support, and the weakening of the two colonial powers, Great Britain and France, all contributed to the victories (sometimes partial and
other times total) of nationalist movements in countries such as Syria,
Lebanon, Egypt, and Iraq. The defeat of Iranian nationalism, symbolized
by Mossadegh, in 1953 was an isolated incident that in no way slowed
down the impetus of the two varieties of Arab nationalism, Ba'athism and
Nasserism, which were to enjoy their moment of glory.

*Nasserism* can be characterized by its resistance to the influence of either bloc. Nasser's doctrine of "positive neutralism" elaborated after the
Bandoeng conference (1955), responded to the region's aspirations for in-

dependence. Nasser became the most popular man in the Middle East as a result of the first arms deal ever concluded with a Communist country and the nationalization of the Suez Canal company, both moves being perceived as challenges to the West. The Syrian-Egyptian union of 1958 marked the apogee of Nasserism as a movement to mobilize the Arab world against the hegemonic ambitions of outside powers. It was in this period that Nasser denounced the Iraqi regime of General Kassem who, although a nationalist like himself, had the fault of being too close to the USSR. The decline of Nasserism began with the break-up of the Syrian-Egyptian union at the end of 1961. The later elaboration of a doctrine which associated socialism with Arab unity, breathed new life into Nasserism, although not enough to assure its survival in the wake of the debacle of June 1967. After Nasser's death, Egypt again became Egyptian, before foundering in an isolation which clearly symbolizes the end of an era.

*Ba'athism* appeared to be better endowed for success than Nasserism. Theoretically, the assets of the movement's founder, Michel Aflak, were superior to those of the leader of the Egyptian revolution, and, from its very beginning right after World War II, the Ba'ath adopted an ideology that synthesized pan-Arabism and socialism and built up a structured organization. What the movement lacked was a charismatic leader of a powerful country, a role that could have been played by Nasser if the Syrian-Egyptian union had lasted. Its failure proved to be of major importance for the ultimate evolution of the nationalist movement: it demonstrated that the ideal of Arab unity was only a utopia. Indeed, all "marriages" since concluded between Arab countries either have not been consummated or have been settled in divorce, thus confirming the sterility of pan-Arabism, at least for the forseeable future.

The actual exercise of power by the Ba'ath since 1963 in Syria and in Iraq has accelerated the decline of the movement in these countries, as it has in the rest of the Arab world. The party, which was firmly resolved to be democratic in nature, has, in fact, relied and continues to rely on the army and security forces to preserve its power. The persistent feud between Damascus and Baghdad illustrates the failure of the Ba'ath's pan-Arab ideology, and the recent "union" between Syria and Libya will not help to blur this image in the eyes of Arab public opinion, which has learned its lesson from repeated past failures. Futhermore, "socialism" as practiced in the two Ba'athist states, where members of the "nouveaux riches" and millionaires are engaging in unbridled speculation, cannot be expected to serve as a model for those who are seeking to establish greater social justice.

The backward slip of the nationalist movement in all its forms confirms the conclusions of Mohammed Hassanein Haykal, the main theoretician of Nasserism, who stated in *Le Monde* of July 1, 1980: "Therefore, while the fifties and sixties were the grand era of the nationalist revolution, the seventies were the era of retrenchment." However, contrary to what might have been expected, Marxism, the other secular ideology in fashion in the Middle East just after World War II, did not succeed in offering an alternative to nationalism.

II. *Communist Movements.* Communism sprang up in the Middle East after the victory at Stalingrad (February 1943), which galvanized many nationalist intellectuals. They turned away from the virtually defeated Axis powers and began to see a potential ally against "western imperialism" in the USSR. During World War II, the Allies had tolerated, and even cooperated with, Marxist groups which in turn were quite disposed to contribute to a victory of the democratic powers then allied with Russia. Communist groups in the Middle East took advantage of this freedom to form cadres and to extend their influence. Thus they played an important and sometimes decisive role after the war. For example, in 1946, Egyptian communists led the nationalist movement directed against the British occupation, particularly among workers and students. The Nasserist junta, which overthrew the monarcy in 1952, included high ranking personalities who were either members of or sympathized with clandestine Marxist organizations. Nasser himself had felt their influence and later applied items from the Communist program (such as agricultural reform, and the nationalization of banks, foreign companies and the Suez Canal) before he actually became resigned to concluding an alliance with the Soviet Union.

Marxists also scored points in countries other than Egypt. Khaled Bagdash, who was then the leader of Arab communism, was elected deputy from Damascus in 1954 at a time when his party numbered among its members or sympathisers people holding key posts in the armed forces. In 1958, Iraqi Communists assisted General Kassem, first in overthrowing the monarchy and then in consolidating his regime; infiltrating the state apparatus, they were in a position, according to most observers, to take over power. The Sudanese Communist party (SCP), which had a solid base among workers and among the peasants of the rich Jazirah province, similarly participated in the October 1964 uprising which brought an end to the military dictatorship of General Abbud. It then associated itself with the junta of General Numeiry, which took control of the country in May 1969 and, in July 1971, the SCP was within a hair's breadth of eliminating its nationalist allies and of usurping power.

Circumstances today are much less favorable to the Communists who, in most cases, have suffered major setbacks. Nasser was able to obtain the self-dissolution of the main Marxist organizations in 1964, in return for only meager compensations; these organizations reconstituted themselves after his death without, however, being able to recover their past vitality. In the Sudan, the SCP has been only a shadow of its former self since the brutal repression that followed the aborted coup d'etat of July 1971. The strength of the Communist Party was also impaired by the severe blows inflicted on it by Ba'ath, particularly in 1963, 1968, and 1978–79. Its association with Saddam Hussein's party in the National Progressive Front from 1973 to 1978 does not seem to have done it much good, any more than the Syrian Communist party has been able to benefit much from the support it continues to give to the government of General Asad. Elsewhere, the groups that champion "scientific socialism" (including those within the Palestinian movement) are marginal or insignificant in their quasi-totality. Notable exceptions to this rule are the Communists of the Yemen Democratic Republic (South Yemen), a Marxist island in a conservative ocean, and the members of the Tudeh party in Iran which is in full development despite the difficult problems it encounters. To some, these two groups appear to be a survival of the past, but to others they are outposts in a territory yet to be conquered.

This is not the place to analyze the multiple causes and variables country-to-country of the general decline of Marxism in the Middle East. Suffice it for the purpose of demonstration to point out that the Communist current has followed more or less the same curve as the nationalist wave in its ebb and flow, leaving an ideological "vacuum" in the Middle East that, it is said today, is destined to be filled by Islam.

III. *The Islamic Movements.* Contrary to those which champion Marxism or nationalism, Islamic movements do not constitute a more or less homogeneous ideological current. The similarities that might be noted, for example, between Saudi Arabian "Wahhabism" and Iranian "Khomeinism" (especially in terms of their rigorous standards of morality) are obviously superficial. The two movements are antagonistic in their respective doctrines and objectives; both are "fundamentalist," in the sense that they claim to apply strictly the teaching of the Quran, and, at the same time, are "revisionist" in the eyes of those who interpret the teaching of the Prophet Muhammed differently. The dividing line in this regard is not that between Sunnis and Shi'is since the Muslim world numbers Sunni Shaiks who lean toward Khomeini while at the same time the Shi'i clergy is deeply divided between partisans and adversaries of the religious and political concepts of Imam Khomeini. In brief, in the opinion of a certain number of Orientalists, the word "fundamentalist" (or "integriste" [i.e. purist] for Francophones) is not a suitable term to designate this or that particular Islamic movement: it would be more realistic, and would clarify the issues at hand, to use the political epithets of conservative and radical in order to distinguish between the two main ideological currents which uphold Islam.

When the expression "the Revival of Islam" is evoked, it usually refers to the second variety, the one which challenges the established order and aims at overthrowing existing regimes, whether they be theocratic or secular. The question in point is to know whether this ideological current has a chance of evolving to the point of offering an alternative to the groups who currently hold power. From a practical viewpoint, it is a question of knowing whether or not Khomeinism is susceptible to expansion beyond the frontiers of Iran. In order to answer this question, it is necessary to examine two aspects of the Iranian revolution.

---

1. *Khomeinism as such, inasmuch as it is an Iranian phenomenon*, is in my opinion difficult to export. The radical wing of the Shi'i clergy in that country, as everybody knows, was able to assume leadership of the popular uprising in 1978–1979, not only because of the political "vacuum" created by the Shah's repression of secular nationalist and Marxist groups, but also and, most important, because of a Shi'i ideology which, in its very essence, challenges temporal power and is hostile to foreign influences; a further reason was the political and sometimes revolutionary role that Iranian mullahs have played historically and especially from the second half of the 19th century onwards. If one adds to that the specific conditions which prevailed during the final years of the Pahlavi regime, and the peculiar personality of Muhammad Reza Shah, it can be argued that the Islamic revolution in Iran is unique and cannot be reproduced in any other country. Of course, it could exert a destabilizing influence in some states which have large Shi'i communities, such as Iraq and Bahrain, but it is highly improbable that, for example, Iraqi Shi'is who are themselves divided could impose their will on the rest of the Iraqi population which includes a strong and reasonably developed Sunni Arab population, Kurds, and other ethnic groups.

2. *However, Khomeinism, inasmuch as it is a Third World ideology*, is eminently contagious under certain conditions. It is not just coincidence that the Islamic revolution in Iran aroused fear, and in some cases panic, in the ruling circles of predominantly Sunni Arab countries from the Atlantic to the Persian Gulf, or that Khomeinism has seduced or enthused

parties, political leaders, and intellectuals in the region despite their secular convictions. Indeed, close examination of the statements and behavior of Imam Khomeini rapidly points to the conclusion that although his ideology is Islamic to a certain extent, its substance is typically nationalist. If one reflects on the often archaic terms he uses to denounce the "great devil" of America, the "diabolic forces" of the West and the East (both rightist and leftist) and those "westernized intellectuals" who "pervert Islam" and oppress the "disinherited" (mostazafin), one realizes that these statements differ little in substance from the diatribes of a Mossadeq, a Nasser, a N'Krumah, or a Sukarno against imperialism, the CIA, multinationals, feudal lords, and agents of neocolonialism. It should be observed that none of those terms are to be found in the sacred texts of Islam, nor is there specified therein the suppression of foreign bases, the nationalization of banks, insurance companies and industrial complexes, or the taking of diplomatic hostages—all of which are, in the eyes of many Islamic leaders, contrary to Islamic ethics and tradition. It is obvious from this that Khomeini, far from being a "fundamentalist," in fact deserves a place in the gallery of Third World secular revolutionaries with whom he shares the Manichean vision of North-South relations and the conviction that the "oppressed masses" will only find their salvation in a return to the sources of their religion, their culture, and their traditions.

Like Nasser, N'Krumah, Trotsky, and other revolutionaries, Khomeini considers his doctrine to be original and to have a scope which is at least supranational, if not universal. Whereas the Egyptian Rais and the Ghanian leader believed they could unite the Arab World and Black Africa respectively against imperialism, the leader of the Iranian revolution aspires to assemble all of the Muslims of Africa and Asia under the banner of *jihad* against local and foreign "oppressors." In other words, Khomeini believes he can succeed where his predecessors failed. It remains to be seen if his emulators outside of Iran will be able to create popular movements at a time when his Islamic Republic projects the image of a country in a state of anarchy, incapable of finding solutions to the political, economic, social, and ethnic problems.


Each one of the countries of the Middle East has its own political traditions and specific conditions which would seem to exclude an Islamic movement's eventually taking power. Egypt, for example, has a long history of secularism and parliamentary activity. The Muslim Brotherhood in Egypt enjoyed its finest hour during the 1940s, and although, after a twenty-year period of decline, it has regained some of its popular appeal

over the past ten years, the fact that the Brotherhood there is faction-
alized tends to lessen its potential influence and, above all, stands in the
way of any hope it may have of power.

The role being played by the Muslim Brotherhood in Syria is much
more important. This is true not so much by reason of its numerical
strength but rather by virtue of the political vacuum in which it is able to
operate. The traditional parties have virtually disappeared, while other,
often clandestine, political groupings are either paralyzed or functioning
in slow motion. We should not be deceived by the terrorist acts of the
Muslim Brotherhood and the responsive chord they strike among the
population: although these acts may appear spectacular they are often inconsequential and, while the politically discontented applaud, they do
not necessarily espouse the ideology or objectives of the terrorists. In my
opinion, this is the situation in Syria, where the enemies of President
Asad are seeking to use the Muslim Brotherhood to destabilize the regime.

The situation in Iraq has come into better focus since the creation, in
November 1980, of a "national front" of an opposition composed of several
Arab and Kurdish parties but excludes any grouping of a confessional
character or leaning. The Shiʿi al-Daʿwa party, which favored Khomeinist
ideology, was not admitted to the front because its preconditions were
judged unacceptable. This exclusion did not happen by chance. Al-Daʿwa
is generally considered a minor party with limited means and one which
has not succeeded in any significant way in mustering and leading the
Shiʿis (approximately 40 percent of the Iraqi population) on a revolutionary course of action. Iraqi Shiʿis tend to prefer membership in other parties, reformist or revolutionary, which are, secular. Of course, the future
may hold something new in store, but, for the present, every indication is
that a change of regime in Baghdad will not be brought about by an Islamic movement.

The armed insurrection in Mecca in November 1979 might lead one to
believe that the Wahhabi monarchy is being threatened by a subversive
force even more fundamentalist than itself. It is true that those who carried out the occupation of the Holy City's Great Mosque denounced the
Wahhabi leaders for being "anti-Islamic." However, the leaders of the insurrection were surrounded by numerous non-Saudis and the population
did not heed their call. Without going so far as to claim that the insurrection did not provoke any sympathy in the public's opinion, one might nevertheless conclude that the potential for popular discontent is not to be
found at the religious level. It is the oil workers, technocrats, women and
merchants who, while remaining attached to Islam, aspire to something
more than strict application of Quranic precepts—to social equality, to

constitutional order, or to moral standards better adapted to their needs in the last quarter of the twentieth century.

In Saudi Arabia, as elsewhere in the Middle East, the seeds of change may be the fruit of an alliance between Islamic and secular forces and between private citizens and the military. As had already been noted, the Iranian revolution is an entirely unique phenomenon. In other countries, the army—led by middle class officers and military strategists—would appear to be just the instrument needed by those who seek to provoke revolutionary change.

The conclusions of this essay flow from the analysis sketched therein. Socio-economic changes, the natural erosion of power, and the aspirations of peoples for more freedom, justice and well-being all contribute to ripen the conditions for change in the political leaderships of the Middle East. Unless the present leaderships show a great capacity to adapt, periods of upheaval appear to be unavoidable during the coming five years. The immobilism or, if you prefer, the stability which the regimes have experienced in recent years, can be ascribed not only to reforms that were consented to and police repression, but also and, most important, to the apparent absence of alternatives. However, it is always possible, as was demonstrated by the Iranian revolution, that major crises can bring to the fore men who are capable of taking over the state apparatus.

External factors can slow down or speed up the dynamics of change. In this respect, the Arab-Israeli conflict deserves a separate study. If we exclude, during the next five years, the prospect of a peace based on compromise which would give even the minimum of satisfaction to the Palestinians to which the Arab countries and the USSR would give their support, a new war or, worse, a continuing impasse, would constitute the most threatening danger for several regimes. Whether or not the oil-producing countries resort to the oil weapon, the consequences might be catastrophic both for the Middle East and for the Western world.

The status quo in the Middle East is cracking. It is not possible to predict where, when, and how it will fall apart. No one expected the Iranian explosion in 1978 nor did anyone forsee the violence of the wave that swept away a monarchy rooted in 25 centuries of history. No doubt it is possible to conceive a variety of scenarios for change, each as plausible as the next. Change may be gradual or abrupt and may direct itself to the right (especially in countries having so-called progressive regimes) or to the left (probably in conservative states tied to the West). In the latter hypothesis, the new leadership that would emerge might practice nationalist and radical politics either secular or religious in nature. Militant Islam, as I have tried to show, does not constitute an ideology in itself but is, rather, a dimension, a component, or a coloration of a Third World movement which is, at present, somnolent but which, by no means, died with Nasserism or Ba'athism.

In a handwritten letter addressed to Nasser in 1965, General de Gaulle maintained that "nationalism is the primary force that shapes the history of nations in the 20th century." Fifteen years later, that message has lost nothing of its actuality.

# Prospects for Stability and New Leadership

## By Michael Sterner

THE FIRST THING I will say about Eric Rouleau's stimulating and perceptive paper is this: at least I agree fully with its first sentence. The Middle East indeed is nothing if not unpredictable. My crystal ball was clouded before the Iraq-Iran war broke out; now it is nearly opaque. Who, for example, would have foreseen even a short time ago the present spectacle of two radical Arab states—Libya and Syria—supporting a non-Arab state—Iran—against a radical Arab "brother." Sorting out the tangle of alliances and counteralliances in the Middle East is difficult enough even for purposes of present-day analysis. Making any kind of assertion as to what all this is going to look like five years hence becomes an almost Nostradamus-like exercise.

If we are to illumine that crystal ball even a little bit, it seems to me that we have to look behind the welter of current events and try to identify some of the more permanent underlying trends at work in the Middle East. In one form or another Eric Rouleau has already touched upon most of the crucial questions. Is the Khomeini revolution an isolated phenomenon with its roots in Iranian nationalism, or does it represent a brand of Islamic fundamentalism that will prove to be the wave of the future for much of the rest of the Islamic world? Does the present assortment of monarchical and "Arab socialist" authoritarian regimes in the Arab world represent a reasonable resting place in the Arabs' search for political and economic systems that suit them, or are they transitional, destined to be swept aside in favor of systems based on more militant ideologies or offering the prospect of more efficient economic management? Will the Arabs find a way of getting their act together or is the present scene of fragmentation and rivalries likely to persist? Is the vast accumulation of wealth, on balance, a stabilizing or destabilizing force?

All of these questions are interrelated in our search for an answer to the bottom-line question: is this area likely to be a congenial one for the pursuit of Western and American interests in the next decade, or is it more likely to be a hostile landscape?

In the time that is available for this presentation, I would like to offer some observations under a couple of these headings in the hope they will expand the areas for discussion that Eric Rouleau has already delineated.

*Islam.* In a world changing at an unprecedented pace and confronting people with problems without clear answers, there is no question that calls for a return to the established verities have a powerful emotional appeal. M. Rouleau correctly makes the point that Khomeini's Islamic absolutism, notwithstanding its Shi'a tinge, has had a resonance among Sunni Moslems far beyond Iran's borders. It is not that the Shi'a/Sunni split has no significance, or that Khomeini's personality or specific policies have all that much appeal outside Iran; it is rather that the Iranian revolution appeared to many outside Iran's borders to give practical vindication to the *idea* that there could be an Islamic alternative to secular government.

Islam has great strengths in this respect. It is more than a religion as we all know; it offers a total life system to its adherents—rules on individual and social behavior, a body of law, a philosophy of government, and even guidelines on economic questions. For more than a thousand years, most of the inhabitants of this region knew no clear distinction between secular and religious authority. Islam's very comprehensiveness enables it to make a strong appeal to those who resent the disappearance of indigenous values and their replacement with "alien" doctrines.

But Islam's comprehensiveness is also its liability. Among the Middle Easterners I am familiar with—mostly Arabs—I have never sensed that fundamental alienation from Western values is a really widespread phenomenon. Quite humanly, Middle Easterners would like if possible to have the best of both worlds—to retain their traditional values and at the same time enjoy the economic, technological, and cultural assets that ties with the West give them. The great majority, I believe, would prefer to solve their problems in a manner that does not require them to choose between the two. Many are concerned at the erosion of traditional values that modernization has wrought, yet few, in the countries I know, are strongly attracted by a remedy that simply offers a wholesale return to the past. When Sadat rather slyly invited Qaddafi about three years ago to come to Egypt to "explain his theories" about Islamic revival to Egyptian groups, the Libyan leader was hooted with derision, most strenuously by an audience of Egyptian women who had been told that they should stick to their homes and be content with the rights Quranic law confers upon them.

Muslim leaders have been notably unsuccessful in defining for the modern Middle Easterner what may reasonably be considered the realm of God, and what reasonably belongs to Caesar. As a result, the Islamic message comes up hard against the practical realities of modern life—and by that I mean not just modern life in Paris or London, but modern life as it is enjoyed or aspired to by the urban classes in the Middle East itself. One hears, for example, that in Tehran it has been decreed that in the new Islamic economy no interest is henceforth to be charged on bank loans. I do not know how Pakistanis or Malaysians are reacting to this, but it is difficult for me to see an idea as nonoperational as this—a measure that would tend to dry up capital flows and cut off economic links with the rest of the world—as having much lasting appeal in the Arab states.

Of course, we need to be cautious in this kind of analysis. We are talking about rational responses, which depend on conditions that offer at least some hope for rational solutions. As we have seen before, rationality can be swept aside in an instant by a wave of primordial emotion when frustrations reach a certain point, and I am keenly conscious that the same kind of arguments could have been put forward—and probably were—to explain why the middle classes in Iran could never allow the country to be swept by an Islamic revolution. All one can say is that after some initial enthuasiasm there is little sign today that, at the two-year mark, the Iranian experience impresses many other Middle Easterners as an attractive model. And, so far at least, political movements in the Arab world that base their messages on Islam have not made much progress in devising a more sophisticated or balanced program that might attract a broader segment of popular support.

*Political and Econonic Systems.* I agree wholeheartedly with Eric Rouleau's comment that one of the salient characteristics of the past decade in the Middle East has been the decline of ideology, both foreign and domestic. Surely it is a notable fact that out of twenty Arab states that have achieved independence, only one, South Yemen, has been governed for any length of time by a Marxist regime, even though there have been literally dozens of changes of government in these countries in the last three decades. The homegrown ideologies that we all worried about in the fifties and sixties—Nasserism, Ba'athism, etc.—similarly, are no longer potent forces on the political scene.

What seems to have happened is that the intense rivalry that characterized the fifties and sixties between republican and monarchical forms, between socialist and free enterprise economies, has settled down into a more restful form of coexistence. There is of course still plenty of bickering going on among these states, but (except for Qaddafi) the bickering is no longer on the basis of Arab socialists calling for the destruction of Arab monarchies. Both Syria and Iraq have better relations with King Hussain and the Saudis than they do with each other. There has been a kind of domestication of the Arab radicals, perhaps partly because these regimes have their hands full with domestic problems, and partly because the traditional forms of government in some areas have proven quite durable. At the same time, most of the traditional regimes have read the handwriting on the wall, and are doing at least something to carry out reforms at a measured pace.

If one looks at the range of existing Arab socialist regimes—Iraq and Syria, Egypt, the Sudan, Algeria—one senses an unmistakable aura of fatigue as far as leadership and policy innovation is concerned. None of these regimes has provided representative government to their people, and none has been notably successful in maximizing economic performance. Yet it is hard to see on the horizon any strong drive toward alternative systems. Neither untrammeled free enterprise nor truly comprehensive statism recommends itself in most of these countries. Few Middle Easterners would wish to see the destinies of their countries at this stage dependent on the vagaries of a really democratic procedure. The difficulties Sadat is having in moving toward more liberal policies on both the political and economic fronts reflect the dilemma that most Middle East countries face. The resistance stems not only from an entrenched bureaucracy, as often reported, but, in my view, also from uncertainty in his own mind as to how far to push this process without doing unacceptable damage to the powers of central leadership.

In a *faute de mieux* sense, authoritarian Arab socialism may represent a system that embodies the kind of compromises that most Arabs see as necessary to cope with the exigencies their nations face, both in the sense of maximizing internal development and in providing reasonable security in a turbulent region. That is not to say that coups or changes of government are unlikely in the next several years. Indeed there could be many, and each will no doubt be accompanied by much beating of drums about how everything will be different—and of course better—than what has gone before. But when the dust settles it would not surprise me to see roughly the same kind of system prevailing in many instances, albeit managed by a new cast of characters.

*Palestinians.* Finally, without meaning to encroach on the territory of the other panel, a word needs to be said about the Palestinian problem and its relationship to regional stability. Israelis are justifiably irritated by the tendency of some Arabs—and perhaps some Western analysts as well—to ascribe the roots of every manifestation of instability in the Middle East to the unresolved Palestinian problem. No one who has a knowledge of the Middle East would assert that once the Arab-Israel conflict is resolved the area will be all peace and stability. But accepting this should not lead us to a mistake in the opposite direction—that of underestimating the Palestinian problem as one of the contributing causes of instability over a much wider area than the immediate arena alone. The Palestinian movement has sufficiently captured the imagination of Arab masses to make any Arab government feel less secure if it is seen to be lukewarm in its support of the Palestinian cause. The movement has also established links with some of the radical philosophies in the area that reach beyond purely Palestinian objectives.

So, in any final assessment of the prospects for area stability, there is a good deal riding on whether a peace process can be constructed that will offer hope to at least moderate Palestinians that a decent future can be worked out for them. Without such hope the Palestinian community will be dominated by militants who will act as a potent destabilizing force over much of the area.

*Conclusion.* What thread can be drawn out of these comments? I am sure the Middle East will remain a turbulent area, with internal stresses and intraregional conflicts exacerbated by the enormous infusions of wealth that are uniquely characteristic of this region. That wealth, as Eric Rouleau has rightly pointed out, acts to tear down the traditional elements of society and increase the trauma of finding new patterns that have some indigenous roots and are not merely imports from abroad. Yet the availability of great wealth can also make pragmatic solutions possible for these countries in some situations that would not be available to poorer parts of the third world. One can hardly project stability for the Middle East in the sense that there will be no changes in government, no crises with Washington in specific cases, or a totally trouble-free environment for investments. Yet I am tempted by the view that, with half a break, the great preponderance of the countries in the area will cope with the problems of making their way in the modern world without resorting to ideologies or a religious fundamentalism that purport to offer sweeping solutions, or that force them to cut off their links with the West.

# American Policy Toward the Arab-Israeli Conflict

## By William B. Quandt

President Ronald Reagan, much like his predecessors, will inherit a lengthy agenda of pending foreign policy problems. Somewhere on that list—near, but not at the top—will be the Arab-Israeli conflict. Much that happens in the Middle East in coming years will stem from how the new Administration chooses to deal with that issue, and where it ultimately figures in the scale of priorities.

Even within the Middle East region, the Arab-Israeli conflict is unlikely to be viewed as the most urgent or most dangerous problem. With a protracted war underway between Iran and Iraq in the Persian Gulf, a preoccupation with rebuilding U.S. military strength in the region, urgent Saudi arms requests, Syrian threats to Jordan, and rising oil prices, the Palestinian issue is very likely to be relegated to the back-burner—at least for a while.

Apart from these current events, there is a more fundamental shift of views about the Middle East among U.S. policy analysts that will most likely have some effect on how the search for peace between Israel and its Arab neighbors is pursued. The main ingredients of the emerging consensus, especially in the Reagan entourage, seem to be the following:

The Soviet threat to the Middle East, and especially to the oil-rich Persian Gulf, is the major problem confronting U.S. foreign policy. To meet this threat, the United States needs a significant increase in its military capabilities to act in the Indian Ocean/Persian Gulf region. Egypt, Israel, and a number of other countries in the region are acquiring strategic importance because of the facilities, and possibly bases, that they can offer to the United States to meet military contingencies. The United States and its allies must be prepared for the eventuality of large-scale disruptions in the supply of oil from the Persian Gulf. The Arab-Israeli conflict, which has long been at the center of Middle East diplomacy, is declining as a source of concern for the United States—at least as long as Egypt and Israel remain at peace.

40

These elements of the new consensus remain very general in scope. Many difficult questions remain to be answered, and often have not even been addressed. Still, the contrast between these underlying assumptions and those that have dominated American policy for the past fifteen years is significant.

After a series of policy setbacks in the 1950s, U.S. Middle East experts began to pay increasing attention to the political dynamics of the area itself. They tried to anticipate political currents in the area and to devise policies that would protect American interests in a Middle East that was undergoing rapid change as a result of decolonization, nationalism, and economic growth. On balance, American diplomats had confidence that the United States could identify itself with the various currents of nationalism sweeping the Middle East, whether they took the form of Arab nationalism in its somewhat romantic form or the more narrowly defined nationalisms of the various entities that were consolidating their existence as independent states. Despite all the problems the United States faced in the area, it was still believed that nationalism would help prevent Soviet domination of the Middle East. Marxism-Leninism as an ideology did not seem to have much appeal to the region.

By contrast, the United States had a history of relatively benign involvement in the Middle East, no colonial past, a dynamic culture, and an immense storehouse of technology and goods. Eventually, it was believed, many Middle East states would find that the United States had more to offer than the Soviet Union. Time was essentially on our side, provided that we remained sensitive to regional political currents. Among other things, it was believed that the establishment of American military bases in the region would be an error. The Soviet setback in Egypt in 1972 confirmed the belief that Moscow's position in the region was vulnerable, that foreign military bases were political irritants, and that nationalism provided a shield against Soviet penetration.

The new consensus that is emerging places less emphasis on nationalism as a force that can be made compatible with American interests. In fact, it is widely believed that nationalism in the Middle East is either a somewhat artificial force, or can only thrive by being anti-Western. A bewildering variety of ethnic groups seem to be asserting their own separate identities. In Washington, pundits are thinking more about the revival of Islam or the prospects for a Middle East composed of numerous minority communities. Some speak wistfully of a U.S.-led Islamic alliance against the Soviet Union. However unrealistic that may seem, there are few analysts who now believe that Arab nationalism is the wave of the future or a force with which the United States can easily identify.

In addition to this change in assessment of the dominant ideological current in the Middle East, the United States seems to lack confidence that it can play a decisive role in resolving most regional conflicts. In the past, it was generally believed that Soviet influence in the Middle East was largely a product of Moscow's ability to exploit regional tensions. The prime example was the ability of the Soviet Union to gain influence in Arab countries by backing Egypt, Syria, and the Palestinians in their confrontation with Israel.

The Arab-Israeli conflict was not the only source of instability in the region. There was also the Turkish-Greek dispute over Cyprus, the India-Pakistan conflict over Kashmir, the Moroccan-Algerian argument over the future of the Western Sahara, and the Somali-Ethiopian conflict over the Ogaden. In each case, the United States was torn between pressures for involvement on one side of the dispute, with the risk of losing influence with the other party, or of remaining aloof and appearing to be irrelevant to the political dynamics of the area. Meanwhile, the Soviets showed little hesitation in pouring arms into such volatile settings when the opportunity to do so arose.

The standard proposed remedy for countering Soviet influence in these circumstances was for the United States, drawing on its political, economic, and military strength, to push for negotiated settlements of regional conflicts. In the absence of armed confrontations, it was believed, the Soviet Union would have fewer advantages in the competition for influence. As a result, the United States at various times launched peace initiatives on the Arab-Israeli issue, on the Cyprus conflict, and tried to contain disputes elsewhere.

More recently, there has been a tendency to believe that these regional disputes are both inevitable and, in any case, only marginally responsible for the growth of Soviet influence in the region. Despite the successful U.S. role in promoting the Egyptian-Israeli peace treaty, the United States has shown little confidence in its ability to bring about a Palestinian settlement, to say nothing of a resolution of the problems of Cyprus, the conflict between India and Pakistan, the war in the Sahara, or the Ogaden confict. Instead of relying primarily on diplomacy to deal with these issues, there is now a tendency to look to the military equations, and most importantly the U.S.-Soviet balance, as the key to regional stability. Arms transfers to U.S. allies are designed to offset Soviet influence, but relatively little corresponding effort is made on the diplomatic front to defuse tensions. As a result, the new consensus tends to reverse the order of priority of the past, arguing that the military balance is of primary importance, and that diplomatic efforts can only be successful once the military equation is favorable to the United States.

Formerly, it was generally believed that the military balance was adequate, and the key to American influence in the region was skillful diplomacy which would keep the Soviets from manipulating regional disputes to their own advantage. The concern of the past was less that the Soviets could force their way into the area than that they would be invited in by one party or another to a conflict. Today, there is considerably more worry about direct Soviet military moves into the Persian Gulf, a fear greatly heightened by the Soviet invasion of Afghanistan in December 1979.

As part of this tendency away from seeing the Middle East in terms of regional politics, the Arab-Israeli conflict is becoming less central to American strategy in the region. A solution, however much desired, is thought to be less essential than in the past. As long as Egypt is at peace with Israel, and the Soviet Union is not physically present in Egypt, the danger of an Arab-Israeli war is greatly diminished. An inadvertent U.S.-Soviet confrontation is therefore unlikely, as is a politically motivated cutback in oil production by Saudi Arabia. This, at least, is the reassuring vision of the new generation of American Middle East strategists.

During his campaign for the Presidency, Mr. Reagan was outspoken in his enthusiasm for Israel. He defined Israel as "a major strategic asset to America," and stated that American aid to Israel is an investment in our own security, not a case of charity. Some of Mr. Reagan's advisors spoke publicly of the desirability of having American bases in Israel, or at the Israeli-constructed air bases in Sinai. Some have fantasized in public about scenarios in which Israeli forces would seize Saudi oil fields in the event of a future energy crisis. On balance, Reagan's inclinations and those of his advisors seem to move him in the direction of a strong commitment to Israel as a strategic asset of the United States in the Middle East. Presumably this would mean even more generous economic and military assistance, and possibly an attempt to develop bases in Israel for American military forces.

While generally supportive of the Camp David approach to peace negotiations, Reagan seems to be open-minded concerning the "Jordanian option." In his September 3, 1980 speech, Reagan was critical of the Camp David Accords for their ambiguity, arguing that UN resolution 242 should be the basis of peace making and that Jordan's participation in the negotiations would be a major step forward. This happens to coincide with the perspective of the Israeli Labor Party, which suggests the interesting possibility that Reagan might feel more comfortable with the Israeli Labor Party in power than with the more conservative Mr. Begin.

Reagan is flatly opposed to an independent Palestinian state, although he has not felt obliged to deal with the issue in any detail. He is opposed to including the PLO in any peace negotiations unless the PLO fundamentally changes its policy on Israel's existence. He has branded the PLO as a terrorist organization, while distinguishing the PLO from the refugees, for whom he shows some concern. One senses that Mr. Reagan would be disinclined to deal with Palestinians of any sort, whether PLO or otherwise. This would be consistent with his apparent preference for talking with Jordan on matters concerning the West Bank.

Concerning the U.S. role in any peace negotiations, Reagan has warned against an activist attempt by Americans to impose their views on Israel and the neighboring Arab states. He seems to view the U.S. role as limited to offering "good offices."

In contrast to the Carter Administration, Reagan and his advisers speak as if they believe there are few links between the Arab-Israeli conflict, broader regional stability, and matters involving oil. This may simply be political convenience, or it may reflect conviction. If the latter, one would anticipate little effort to press for an Arab-Israeli settlement.

Turning from Mr. Reagan's predispositions to the situation he will find in the Middle East as he tries to fashion a strategy for peace, one sees that Reagan's reticence to become involved in the Palestinian question is likely to be reinforced by the unusual complexity of the regional political scene. First there is the fact that both Israel and Egypt remain committed to the stalemated Camp David approach to negotiations. This is particularly true of Prime Minister Begin, but even President Sadat is anxious that any alternative to Camp David be seen as an outgrowth of his strategy, not a repudiation of it.

The Israeli picture is clouded by the existence of a shaky coalition at present and the prospect of elections by November 1981 at the latest. Some analysts believe that Mr. Begin's only chance of winning the election resides in his ability to exploit a U.S.-Israeli crisis to his advantage or to persuade Israeli voters that his hard-line policies are the only defense against overwhelming U.S.-Egyptian pressure for concessions. If this is believed, and if Mr. Reagan hopes to deal with a Labor government, he will probably go out of his way to avoid arguments with Mr. Begin. Sadat may agree to follow suit, in which case Camp David talks will at most become a formal ritual, pending Israeli elections.

If the Labor Party does come to power, it will find itself in one of two conditions. With unprecedented good luck, it might win an absolute majority, in which case it would have no need for coalition partners and could offer significant territorial concessions to Jordan in negotiations. But if Labor is obliged to include the National Religious Party in the government, it will have much less flexibility. In either case, the best offer that Labor can possibly make is likely to fall considerably short of anything King Hussein can accept.

If Israel's flexibility is certain to be limited on questions of future borders and Jerusalem, so also will Jordan's room for maneuver. Jordan has done remarkably well and is escaping from its isolation of the early 1970s, and it can probably count on some support from Saudi Arabia and Iraq if it chooses to join the negotiating process. But Hussein will have nothing to do with Camp David as it has been interpreted by Begin. Instead, he will prefer to explore the outer limits of the Labor party's willingness to meet his essential criteria of territorial withdrawal. If Jordan does become involved in peace talks, Hussein will have to anticipate serious pressures from the Syrians and some elements of the PLO.

Given the political constraints on both Israel and Jordan, it will be difficult to move toward a peace settlement all in one step. The Camp David approach envisaged an interim stage of "autonomy" for the Palestinians. A new initiative might be built around an interim stage of partial Israeli withdrawal from the populated areas of the West Bank. For this to work on the Arab side there would have to be some apparent link to further withdrawal, to an Arab role in part of Jerusalem, and to some symbolic satisfaction of Palestinian rights.

While the prospect of going beyond the Camp David approach seems to hold out some possibility that the stalemate of 1980 may be broken, the Reagan Administration will face a number of crucial tests before it will have the chance to test the opportunities for peace. Israel, Saudi Arabia, Jordan and Egypt will all be anxious to win early support from Mr. Reagan for their positions.

Israel will want to get Mr. Reagan to repeat his views on the legality of settlements in occupied territories. Some Israeli extremists may press for annexation of the Syrian Golan Heights in hope that Mr. Reagan will acquiesce in a fait accompli. Also, the explosive situation in Lebanon will tempt the Israelis to strike at PLO bases and the Israelis will watch to see Mr. Reagan's reaction.

The Saudis will also be after Mr. Reagan to provide evidence of support. One test will involve long-deferred requests for sophisticated arms to enhance the effectiveness of the 60 F–15 aircraft that will begin to arrive in 1981. A second test, perhaps more easily deferred than requests for arms, will be aimed at influencing U.S. policy toward the Palestinian question. At a minimum, the Saudis will want Mr. Reagan to adhere to long-standing U.S. positions on Jerusalem, Israeli settlements, and the applicability of UN Resolution 242 to all fronts of the conflict. The public assertion of an independent U.S. position on these issues will count nearly as much as actual progress toward a comprehensive peace settlement.

Finally, Jordan can be expected to try to impress upon the Reagan administration the central role that it can play in both Gulf affairs and in the Arab-Israeli arena. In the aftermath of border tensions with Syria in December 1980, the Jordanians will certainly press the new administration for accelerated delivery of arms.

In brief, Reagan has an opportunity to develop a credible peace strategy for the Middle East. But to do so, he will have to take the issue seriously, capturing the nuances of the problem in a way that his rhetoric to date has not reflected. He will also need to appreciate the political nature of the conflict, not just its military dimensions. That realization must be coupled with an appreciation of the need for American diplomatic leadership if the Palestinian impasse is to be broken. And he will have to understand the subtle ways in which U.S. prestige and credibility in the Gulf depend upon the position taken on the Arab-Israeli conflict.

Perhaps most difficult of all, Reagan will have to find a way to maintain the confidence of Egypt and Israel, while at the same time improving relations with Saudi Arabia, Jordan and moderate Palestinians. Mr. Reagan will enjoy a brief period of goodwill during which he can put his own stamp on American Middle East policy. How he uses that time, and how he tries to strike a balance among the various dimensions of U.S. interests in the Middle East, will probably determine the course of American policy for most of his incumbency.

# An Alternative View of the Arab-Israeli Conflict

### By Stephen S. Rosenfeld

I SEE THE FORCE in Bill Quandt's argument that considerations of oil and power in the Persian Gulf will overtake recent American concern with what can be seen in one light merely as the interminable squabbling of two small peoples, Israelis and Palestinians, along the Mediterranean coast. The strategic logic is evident if you weigh the demonstrable importance to the U.S. of Western access to Gulf oil. Certainly the war between Iran and Iraq, being the first of the various tumultuous events in that region since the 1973 embargo to impinge on the flow of oil, has freshened the case for priority attention to the Gulf. Certainly the Israelis will second that motion, making the self-evident argument that they had nothing to do with the oil clot this time. Certainly many Americans, scared as they are by rumblings of peril around the Gulf, are of a mind to believe it.

But I don't believe it—rather, it's far from a sure thing. It will not happen unless the key actors wish it to happen or allow it to happen. There is a logic at work but not an iron logic, merely the changeable logic of men.

Let me deal first with the most obvious factors—that Palestinian agitation will not cease, that a Palestinian card will remain on the table available for inter-Arab play, and that the countries must vulnerable to Palestinian pressure include the major oil producers of the Gulf. I find it hard to believe that concerned Arabs will allow American strategic priorities to be the sole determining factor in setting the agenda for the Middle East. Furthermore, the oil dependence which gives the Palestinians' Arab sponsors most of their clout will linger through the decade. In short, too much has happened to turn back the Palestinian clock.

The argument will be that Americans cannot expect full, or fuller, Arab cooperation in coping with geopolitical calamity in the Gulf, despite the fact that some of the Arabs withholding cooperation may pay heavily as a result, *if* Americans are not more forthcoming on the Palestinian question. Some part of this contention will always be rhetoric or blackmail and should either be ignored or faced down. But some part will also be legitimate, or arguable, and it will be carried forward not only by Arabs but

47

also by the various Americans who are engaged now in the Palestinian issue.

Their number includes, beyond a handful of Palestinians, diplomats hoping to ease America's way, strategists wanting that extra edge, businessmen looking for a profit, intellectuals seeking truth (or power), Zionists (a few anyway) hoping to make Israel more secure and to perfect their vision of Zionism, anti-Zionists hoping to make Israel less secure or to perfect their vision of Zionism, plus assorted radicals, church people, and others. A motley crew? Yes, but an increasingly important one. An interesting measure, by the way, of the extent to which the Palestinian question has invested the American public scene is that an actress could get herself on the cover of a national magazine earlier this fall essentially for being a supporter of the PLO.

Perhaps the relevant question is whether a concern for the Palestinian issue is necessarily incompatible with a parallel concern for the strategic equation. I can see a calculating Israel "selling" itself as a strategic partner, and perhaps offering its real estate, for a price which would include a go-slow American attitude on the West Bank. However, I can also see an anxiety-ridden Israel finding in America's strategic company the extra measure of assurance it needs to take the risks unavoidably associated with a Palestinian settlement. The disengagement accords and the Israeli-Egyptian peace treaty ought to reassure those who fear that Israel will simply pocket the aid and arms and run. My point is that strategic considerations need *not* inhibit the U.S. from pressing for an Israeli-Palestinian solution. Handled carefully, those considerations may even have an opposite, door-opening effect.

But there is a less obvious set of factors at work which have to do with the inner dynamics of the Israeli-Palestinian conflict. A common premise is that only the pressure of outsiders can bring the parties into some sort of coexistence; another is that this pressure cannot or will not be applied if the outsiders are overly distracted; and still another is that left more or less to themselves, both Israelis and Palestinians will merely allow their dispute to fester. These have become more widely held since the Egyptian-Israeli peace treaty would seem to have all but removed the prospect of another general Arab-Israeli war. That the Arab-Israeli dispute has seemingly lost its powderkeg potential is, regrettably, a cause of real remorse for some Americans, who feel that only the prospect of World War III could conceivably budge the United States out of its pro-Israel trance.

No matter, there is a model of Israeli-Palestinian intractability. It is sustained on the one hand by the Palestinian belief that Israel is a foreign intrusion thrust upon the Arab heartland by Westerners who could, but won't, force Israel to shrivel, if not to disappear. It is sustained on the other hand by the Israeli belief that the Palestinian question is an artificial one kept alive by Arabs (and others), an instrument in their rivalries and a pawn to their abiding desire to eliminate the Jewish state.

Merits aside, are the implications of this model accurate, or automatic, or acceptable? If the relevant outsiders are distracted by matters of oil, geopolitics and what have you, *will* Israelis and Palestinians invariably turn away from their principal *mutual* labor of the last few years? I would define this labor an an unprecedented concentration in public and in private on the terms on which they might, or might not, live side by side. Is there no alternative or supplement to the active, attentive, expensive, nervewracking, pushy, carrot-and-stick diplomacy practiced by Americans on Israelis, and by Arabs on Palestinians? These days many Palestinians fear that there is no alternative, many Israelis hope so, and the MERI analysis distributed to us suggests so.

However, let us not be so sure. Let us keep in mind, with all due respect to the differences, the breakthrough potential, long unsuspected but suddenly revealed on the Egyptian-Israeli front. Furthermore, consider the Palestinians, who have so far relied heavily on leverage applied by others on Israel to bring it closer to their political goals. Suppose that, in the wake of the Iran-Iraq war, Palestinians realized they could not expect most other Arabs to be as demanding on *their* behalf on the United States as those Arabs were before the war. Suppose the Palestinians were to come to feel the cool of great-power inattention and to see their choice in terms of either accepting the fruits of a Jordanian-Labor Party negotiation, which would initially mean less than the full West Bank and less than full independence, or expect nothing for a further indefinite period. Suppose some of the Palestinians' *proven* friends were to commend acceptance of this course to them. Suppose the Israelis were to learn on the ground that such a step did not endanger their security, and, indeed, enhanced it.

Here I must defend myself against the charge of being a Pollyanna. I don't predict all of this will happen. I am simply saying, by way of outlining an alternative analysis, that it could happen if the two parties, left pretty much to themselves, were to take small steps, with its being understood that no single small step could be regarded necessarily either as a stepping stone or as a stopping place. The negotiation could begin with gestures, such as a decision by Arafat to receive a Zionist member of the Knesset (do you think he would ever do that?), or a decision by the Israelis to permit the return of some expelled Palestinian mayors (would *they* do that?). I have long been intrigued by Dayan's idea of a unilateral pullback of the Israeli military administration in the West Bank. The Gaza-first tactic might also have some ice-breaking potential. But who knows? Both sides would have to head down a road the end of which was not in sight—that is, the Camp David uncertainty without the Camp David structure.

Why would they do it? The Israelis would do it because Israel is a nation in permanent fateful crisis—a nation being drained of its idealism as well as of its resources and its very independence, a gasping nation. But I deeply believe it is still a nation that has not lost the "sweet" Zionist vision of accommodation. The 100th birthday of Zeev Jabotinsky was observed in New York recently at a dinner addressed by Menahem Begin. I prefer to believe that this was not a revival of Jabotinsky (to me the fount of "sour" Zionism), but his last hurrah. As for the Palestinians, they would do it because they too are in a situation contrived of equal parts of desperation and hope.

The Israelis are conceivably merely one election away from a strong Labor government, without the NRP, that, I think, will make King Hussein an offer he will have to consider seriously—an offer to liberate a million Palestinians from Israeli rule. There are two chief rabbis in Israel and they differ on whether God meant the Jews to keep the West Bank if peace were at stake. That says enough about Israeli ambivalence. In my opinion, no one who views the political distance that the PLO has come can look at that organization now and say it cannot possibly go the relatively small distance remaining. One piece of evidence I would cite to support this view is the continuing Palestinian debate, up and down, over whether to revise certain charter provisions that, if implemented, would have the effect of removing Israel from the political map. Another piece of evidence is the continuing strain of Palestinian interest in a relationship with Jordan, and not just in an "independent" West Bank ministate.

To be sure, these comments run against the grain of the historical pessimism that permeates most political analysis of the Mideast. There is a whole school of Zionism—Jabotinsky's, Begin's—that anticipates implicitly, sometimes explicitly, perpetual conflict leading to a possible apocalypse. And there is a parallel school—Habash's, Qaddafi's—of Palestinianism. There is also a whole school of *commentary* on Zionism—shall we call it a particular Arabist school?—that stresses what is called the alien, exclusivist, racist, expansionist, militaristic nature of Zionism. There is, again, a parallel school of commentary on Palestinianism, centering on the concept that Palestinian nationalism is merely the latest expression of true, total, genocidal anti-Semitism.

I am not here trying to summon up the kind of pox-on-both-your-houses evenhandedness that disguises a bias for the status quo. I am simply trying to indicate that all of us should be aware of the arbitrary element (not the only element) in much analysis. We should not be making excuses for immobilism or gratuitously spoiling the atmosphere, which is important in the Middle East and which is already spoiled enough. This is no plea for simplemindedness and flight from history. It is not even a plea for the kind of unreasoning, crazy, stubborn, almost perverse personal religious optimism by which Jimmy Carter staggered most of the experts—though surely none of you—and brought off an Egyptian-Israeli peace. I would just like to point out that it is easy, and sometimes fashionable, to see the down side and we should not all be crowded over there.

Ronald Reagan, I would say, is no down-sider. What is he? His public statements, the spread of his advisers on the Mideast issue, and the weight of the constituencies he would presumably serve all point in various directions. At this point I would not want to try to read much from the tea leaves. His general inclination to take a second look at the Camp David emphasis on Palestinian autonomy is important and, more important still, is his evident readiness to step back from the Carter precedent of intense personal presidential involvement in Mideast affairs. For Reagan this might be as much a matter of temperament as of strategy. In either event the effect could be to give more play to the internal dynamics that I have been underlining here.

# The Soviet Union and the Middle East

## By William G. Hyland

ONE BY-PRODUCT of the dual crises in the Persian Gulf and Afghanistan has been the dramatic reminder they provided of the historic Russian interest in the area "south of Batum"—one of the more ominous-sounding phrases plucked out of the Soviet-German negotiations in 1940. Indeed, the Persian Gulf is frequently cited as the "focal point" of Soviet ambitions. While there is something to be said for drawing historical analogies, the current crisis cannot be easily explained or dismissed as the resumption of age-old Russian designs. It is necessary to put the current crisis in the perspective of the evolution of the Soviet policy of the past several years.

The Soviet entry into the Arab world in 1955 was opportunistic in almost every sense. The USSR was invited, without much effort on its part. Nasser wanted a counterweight to Western power and the USSR was the natural choice. It was an opportunity to leapfrog the growing encirclement of the USSR which was the aim of the Dulles alliance systems. Furthermore, internally, Khrushchev himself wanted to reduce the influence of Molotov in the Politburo and enhance that of his own protege, Dimitri Shepilov.

Beyond sheer opportunism, it is difficult to ascribe any precise objectives or a master plan to the Soviets. Indeed, Soviet policy bears the characteristic of considerable improvisation. There was no "theory" for alignment with noncommunist anti-Western regimes, even though Lenin had dimly perceived that the anticolonial period would lead to an intensification of revolutionary upheavals. Neither was there a program for advancing the interests of local communists who suffered varying fates in the Arab world, nor was any clear military advance to be expected. One irony in the situation is that, at the very time Khrushchev was launching a thrust into the Middle East, he was sacking his chief of naval operations who favored building a blue water navy.

In the decade that followed, what gradually emerged was a strategy of denial—that is, a major effort by the Soviet Union to deny the Middle

East, North Africa and South Asia to American and Western influence. The principal instruments used were military aid, economic assistance, and a highly pragmatic attitude toward indigenous ideologies and political structures.

By 1965–66, the original phase of Soviet intervention had about run its course. The vague hopes of infiltrating and influencing the development of Arab regimes from within had clearly failed, but the broad strategy of denial had worked beyond expectations. It seemed that the area stretching from Algeria to Afghanistan might be ripe for a new policy, namely, conversion into a genuine Soviet sphere of influence or, in other words, a sort of loose alliance system. By 1969 events had progressed to the point that Kosygin boldly advanced a prospect for an agreement on regional cooperation between the Soviet Union, Afghanistan, Pakistan, India and Iran. Soviet policy was showing unmistakable signs of what the Chinese are fond of calling "hegemonism."

It may well be that the Soviet Union could and would have developed this strategy had it not been interrupted by the effects of the Arab-Israeli War. The Soviets played a role in encouraging the outbreak of the Six Day War by passing on warnings to the Arab states of an impending Israeli attack. If they had not actually wanted a war, they certainly miscalculated. Moscow underestimated the volatility of the area and overestimated Arab military capabilities. The stunning Arab defeat served to demonstrate the limits of Soviet policy and the potential weakness in relying entirely on Soviet arms and diplomacy. Indeed, there was sharp criticism of Soviet policies in the Arab world, and also a dispute within the Soviet leadership about the overly prudent policies of Brezhnev and Kosygin which led to the removal of one high level leader (the head of the Moscow Party) and the downgrading of others.

The upshot was that the Soviets were thereby under far greater pressure to demonstrate that Arab demands on Israel could be advanced under Moscow's auspices. In the course of promoting this general line, Soviet policy had to align itself increasingly with the more radical elements in the anti-Israeli struggle and to accept the PLO as a legitimate political entity and instrument.

In this period, the Soviets began to lose control of events. While they cooperated with the U.S. in sponsoring U.N. Resolution 242, and in launching the mission of Gunnar Jarring in 1968, the Soviets were buffeted by Nasser's diplomacy and increasingly dragged into a confrontation policy along the Suez canal.

The Soviets, by significantly increasing their military involvement, could check Israeli pressure as happened in the confrontation of 1970.

However, Soviet policy could not convert this temporary advantage into political gain. When superpower diplomacy eventually broke down and when Nasser died, the Soviets were driven to adopt new expedients to shore up their relationship with Egypt, especially the signing of a friendship treaty in 1971. The treaty, according to a message from Brezhnev to Sadat, was to be a "significant means of pressure on Israel and the U.S., who now confront the U.A.R. in its struggle to achieve its legitimate rights. . . ." In fact, by the time it was actually signed, during a hurried visit by then-President Podgorny, the treaty was an anticlimax; Sadat had succeeded in purging his pro-Soviet colleagues, particularly Ali Sabri.

Perhaps more important was that the general line of Soviet foreign policy was shifting toward a new relationship with the U.S., towards what became known as the period of detente. Of even greater priority than the struggle in the Middle East was the Soviet obsession with obtaining political ratification of their position in East and Central Europe. This process began to develop in negotiations with the new West German government of Chancellor Willy Brandt. By August 1970, the first Soviet-German treaty had been signed, followed by a Berlin settlement with the U.S., Great Britain and France in 1971, and a breakthrough in SALT negotiations with the U.S. Furthermore, following the the secret Kissinger trip to Peking, there was quick agreement on a Soviet-American summit in Moscow for May 1972, and this meeting was to prove to be a turning point in Soviet Middle Eastern policy.

Sadat's disenchantment, arising from Soviet failure to use the Nixon summit to put pressure on Israel through the U.S., led directly to his decision to expel Soviet advisors from Egypt. It was also the first step toward inviting the return of American power to the area. In the wake of the initial break with Sadat, the Soviets adopted a highly ambivalent course that had as its inexorable outcome the encouragement of the war in October 1973. On the one hand, the Soviets tried to win back their position by agreeing to new Egyptian military demands and, on the other hand, they adopted a policy of agitating more vigorously for political settlement. The irony was that they also demonstrated the limits of their ability to make political progress.

The nature of Soviet behavior on the eve of, and during, the Yom Kippur War is still being debated. Suffice it to say that the Soviets did little to stop the drift of events. Once hostilities broke out they played a highly opportunistic hand: at first, they tried to halt the fighting, but then they allowed it to run free on the assumption the Arabs might be gaining; finally, they desperately tried to halt the fighting to stave off a massive Arab defeat. The war was a turning point for Soviet policy. It dealt a blow to the prospects for continuing a "detente" with the U.S. Brezhnev claimed that had it not been for detente, the events might have taken an even more dangerous turn, but nevertheless a backlash and disillusionment was created in the U.S. Moreover, Sadat, and to a lesser extent, Asad, recognized that only the U.S. could deliver any political gains against Israel. American mediation, through the Kissinger shuttle diplomacy, proceeded at the expense of the USSR, and the collapse of the Soviet position in the Arab world inclined the USSR toward more opportunistic policies in other areas. The loss in Egypt was compensated for, to some extent, by new prospects in Africa. The revolution in Portugal led to the termination of the Portuguese empire and to the opening of opportunities for Soviet influence in Mozambique and Angola. Simultaneously, the American position in Ethiopia suddenly collapsed when a radical group of military officers overthrew the Emperor. However, these opportunities for the Soviets were offset, in some degree, by the substantial build-up of Iran as a military power, the enforced rapprochement between Iran and Iraq, the maneuvering of the Daud regime in Kabul, and the troubles of Mrs. Gandhi which led to her fall from power.

In short, the Middle East became submerged in a general international landscape that was becoming extremely fluid and open to new manipulation.

## The New Course

In the period dating from 1975–1976, it appears that Soviet policy in general was reviewed, revised, and redirected in a more aggressive fashion. The change reflected growing scepticism in Moscow about the fruits of detente with the U.S. It also reflected a determination to counter U.S. diplomacy—in effect, once again, a Soviet attempt to break out of what appeared to be a growing alignment of anti-Soviet states, this time China, the U.S., Western Europe and Japan. As for the Middle East, the shift in policy was reflected in the hardening of the Soviet position on the terms for a settlement, particularly its clear stand in favor of Palestinian statehood under PLO auspices, a more rigid insistence on the 1967 borders, and an insistence on a comprehensive settlement in the Geneva process.

As has been pointed out, one effect of Soviet exclusion from the political process of settling the Arab-Israeli conflict was to shift Soviet efforts and attention toward South Asia and the Horn of Africa, where new opportunities presented themselves. In the spring and summer of 1977, the Soviets made an effort to bring its Somali client into a grouping with its old ally in South Yemen and the Ethiopian regime of Col. Mengistu, a new-found ally. President Siad Barre finally rejected this overture, and the Soviets accomplished a major diplomatic revolution by switching their political and military support from Somalia to Ethiopia. At first it seemed that the Soviets had suffered a major political defeat, having once again been expelled by an Arab state. However, it soon became apparent that a new alliance was in the making; moreover, Cuban troops began to shift from Angola to Ethiopia and the Soviet Union embarked on its second major military intervention in Africa, this one under more open and direct Soviet military organization and command. Somalia was defeated by a Cuban offensive modeled on the lines of a Soviet World War II battle.

Meanwhile, in South Yemen, the People's Democratic Republic of Yemen (PDRY), the Soviets were involving themselves more deeply in the internal politics of a state long thought to be deeply under their influence. Despite strong Soviet support and involvement, the president of the PDRY was flirting with the possibility of rapprochement with North Yemen, Saudi Arabia and even the U.S. A series of bizarre events led to a coup in June 1978, in which PDRY President Ali Rubayi was killed. He was replaced by the general secretary of the party, Fattah Ismail. Soviet fingerprints seemed to be all over the affair. Key figures in the coup, the minister of defense and the present prime minister (who later took power from Ismail), were both in touch with Soviet officials in Moscow in the weeks prior to the coup.

Whether by design or not, within a brief period the Soviets had significantly shored up their strategic position in the Horn of Africa and at the straits of Bab El Mandeb, and state treaties were concluded with Ethiopia and later with the PDRY. These developments, at least in retrospect, were signs of a new aggressiveness emanating from Moscow, which were later to be reflected in the Communist coup in Afghanistan. No one, of course, can demonstrate that Moscow was intimately involved in the Afghan coup in 1978, but some observers on the scene have reached that conclusion. (See Theodore Elliot, *Strategic Review*, Spring 1979). In any case, the Soviets promoted a coalition between the Khalq and Parchem factions in Afghanistan in July 1977. Moscow's relations with Daud were becoming frayed, but a proposal to move against him certainly could have been frustrated by the Soviets, since, given the record of loyalty to Moscow subsequently demonstrated by all Afghan communist factions, it is obvious that the coup would not have proceeded over Soviet objections.

Indeed, Moscow not only supported the new communist regime, it made no effort to prevent an internal purge of the Parchem, and it extended major assistance, including a new state treaty signed December 1978. Moscow's miscalculation was that the new government was too doctrinaire and too rigid in its determination to apply "socialism." It succeeded in alienating large segments of the population and, within a year, the situation was deteriorating rapidly and the Soviets were toying with a new coup, this time against the leader of the Khalq, Hafizullah Amin. By July-August 1979, there were rumors of inevitable Soviet intervention. In September 1979, on his return from Havana, and after a stopover in Moscow, Mohammed Taraki apparently launched an abortive coup in which he was killed. Amin tightened his controls, probably against Soviet advice, and eventually the Soviet ambassador was expelled. Meanwhile practical control of the country was slipping from the regime's grasp. The Soviets, having surveyed the situation through a mission of the chief-of-staff of the ground forces, General Pavlovsky, finally had no real choice: either the communist regime in Kabul would disintegrate and be replaced with a chauvinistic, Muslim regime not unlike its counterpart in Iran or, as an alternative, the Soviets could intervene with major forces.

---

The Soviet invasion of Afghanistan was a major watershed event, not only for South Asia, but also for the super power relationship and future Soviet strategy. What does it portend?

First of all, the invasion, along with the collapse of Iran, has created a new geopolitical situation. Pakistan, ally of the U.S. and China, now faces the Soviet Union at the Khyber pass. Regardless of whether or not Soviet motives were "defensive" in sending 100,000 troops into Afghanistan, their presence creates a new situation of peril for Pakistan. Soviet pressures on Pakistan began almost immediately and Pakistan has been the focal point of a Soviet campaign of intimidation, ostensibly because of Pakistan's support for the Afghan guerillas, without a U.S. guarantee. Pakistan has been maneuvering to keep the Soviet Union at bay. But strategically, the Soviets have broader aims: to isolate Pakistan, first by breaking the American-Pak connection as well as Islamabad's link to China; the neutralization of Pakistan was implicit in various schemes promoted by Moscow and Kabul to solve the Afghan crisis. However, beyond this, the Soviets hope gradually to "Findlandize" the Pak regime. The fortuitous return of Mrs. Gandhi was almost instantly exploited by a Soviet arms deal for $1.6 billion (compared to about $200 million offered Pakistan by the U.S.). Moreover, the Soviet military effort on the ground has come closer to involving Pakistani territory: hot pursuit by Soviet helicopters and aircraft became more frequent, so that it appeared that Pakistan "is being sucked slowly into the Afghan quicksand" (*Washington Post*, September 20). Clearly, Pakistan's alternatives are shrinking; to avoid a major clash with the USSR, its course will almost have to move toward some accommodation with Moscow.

*Iran.* Soviet strategy vis-à-vis Iran is more complicated and uncertain. After a period of courting the new revolutionary government, relations soured. The more moderate factions in Iran may have seen the pitfalls in relying on the USSR, especially given its close links to the Tudeh party. However, the attitude of the Muslim fundamentalists has been more ambivalent: publicly, at least, the Soviets have been a distinctly lesser evil than the U.S. But a new phase of the revolution seemed to be consolidating in the fall of 1980 under the new Parliament and new cabinet; tensions with the Soviet Union grew.

*Iraq.* In 1977–78, before the war with Iran, despite tension with Moscow arising from the activities of local communists in Iraq, Soviet relations with Baghdad had not deteriorated significantly. The Soviets were shrewd enough to appreciate that the collapse of Iranian power opened the entire Gulf to domination by another outside power; they probably suspected that the U.S. would begin to move to compensate for its debacle in Iran by making overtures to Iraq, since before the war reports of this new American interest were plentiful. Thus, it seems likely that the Soviets encouraged Iraq's aggressive confrontation with Iran, without, perhaps, counseling an outright attack.

## The Outlook

The outlook for Soviet policy through 1985 is conditioned by three sets of factors: those relating to the Middle East-Persian Gulf area, those relating to internal Soviet politics, economy, and succession, and those relating to general trends in Soviet-American relations.

## Regional Factors

To turn toward the regional factors, first of all, there are two short term situations to be considered: the course of the Afghanistan war and the course of the Iran-Iraq war.

The war in Afghanistan is difficult to analyze because the reporting is so erratic. Soviet advances or setbacks are highlighted from time to time in dubious reporting, mainly from Pakistan and India. However, the trend seems to be that the Soviets are slowly consolidating a military position throughout most of the country and that resistance is diminishing to a low-level guerrilla war. The major problem is that the Soviets cannot build up a legitimate Afghan regime or Afghan army to take on their burdens; thus the Soviets face long-term occupation and the accompanying political consequences of sporadic harrassment (in the UN, or international gatherings). This is well within Soviet tolerance, and, indeed, the Soviets are paying a diminishing price for their strategic gains, largely because the West Europeans have decided not to make Afghanistan a major test case lest "detente" in Central Europe be threatened. In the short term, therefore, the Soviet position in the general area seems to have been significantly strengthened by the conquest of Afghanistan. It puts the Soviets on the flank of Iran and on the strategic approaches to Pakistan, which is now virtually encircled.

How far the Soviets can go in using the Afghan invasion as a stepping stone to further advances now depends in part on the outcome of the war between Iran and Iraq and in part on the evolution of the politics of Iran.

The Soviets have tried to play both sides of the war. Initially, they received a publicized visit from the Iraqi leadership, but balanced this with a bow towards Teheran. This pattern of even-handedness has prevailed, at least on the surface. In fact, the Soviets seemed to have positioned themselves to move in either direction, but their actions suggest a slight preference for Iran over the long term. Even before the war there were strains in their relationship with Iraq. The Soviets had retained a relationship with Syria despite the rising tensions between Damascus and Baghdad. Once the Iraqi attack had been launched, the Soviets made no effort to resupply the Iraqi war effort. And, far more important, they proceeded with a long-delayed friendship treaty with Syria, the centerpiece of a visit to Moscow by Asad. While proclaiming that the treaty was not directed against any third parties, Soviet signature was in itself a humiliation for the Iraqi leadership, which, however, had no choice but to swallow it.

For the Soviets the best outcome would be a gradual dwindling of the conflict, allowing Moscow to retain its position in Iraq and to work for an opening in Iran. If this is in fact the outcome, then, over time, the Soviets will prepare a position from which they can offer Iran their protection as a major outside power against the U.S. This would allow realization of the major aim of neutralizing the entire strategic area covered by Iran, Pakistan, and Afghanistan which, in turn, would give the Soviets additional leverage in the Gulf and a position from which to squeeze Iraq between Iran and Syria.

The ultimate aim of this strategy remains the destabilization of Saudi Arabia. An alignment of Syria, Iran and Libya is a step in this direction. Soviet opportunities for internal subversion in Saudi Arabia are presumably slender, but support of Libya and the PLO will continue to provide a vehicle for indirect Soviet influence. As one authority has noted, the Soviets hope to attack the center (Saudi Arabia) by radicalizing the fringes of the Arabian Peninsula (especially from South Yemen).

An additional Soviet objective is to gain access to Middle Eastern oil, which, however, is probably not an overriding motive, despite speculation in the Western press. The Soviets would have valid strategic objectives, even if there were no oil in the area. But, given their probable requirements for imports of oil by the mid 1980s, the Soviets will want to establish a source of supply from a friendly political regime. Iran, which has lost its markets and a good deal of its physical capabilities, would thus fit both Moscow's economic and strategic objectives. Oil in return for rebuilding the Iranian military machine would seem a natural combination.

## Internal Factors

The increased turbulence in the Middle East comes at a time when the Soviets must face some critical problems of the 1980s. First, there is the matter of their own political succession and second, there are economic choices that must eventually be made by a new leadership.

The outcome of the Soviet succession grows increasingly hazy. An orderly change from Brezhnev has obviously not taken place, and, perhaps, was deliberately deferred or rejected at the politburo level in 1977, when Brezhnev became president and retained his party overlordship. The Party Congress of February 1981 would seem to provide another suitable occasion, but not only is there no sign that he is preparing his successor, but recent promotions suggest a determination to persevere. Naming a crown prince may be politically impossible in any case; in one's political lifetime it is dangerous for both men, and ensuring the line of succession after one's political departure is probably impossible. The odds will grow against the succession as a transition by half steps—that is, from Brezhnev to Kirilenko to a younger man. This is still the most likely path, but the longer it is delayed the less likely it is to be effective. Thus, the odds will grow for a disorderly succession period with frequent shifts in personnel. This introduces an element of great uncertainty. Succession periods, historically, do loosen political boundaries and new ideas are introduced, but the chances of overturning or significantly affecting the general conservatism built up in the Brezhnev era are certainly less than even. The more likely outcome is the continuation of a strong conservative leadership, resting on the support of the party bureaucracy, the military, the KGB, and the heavy industrialists, rather than the emergence of a more "liberal" group drawn from technicians and government bureaucracy. Major economic reform, which might be the central domestic issue, seems less likely in such a constellation of powers.

The economic situation may reach a point, however, where deferring structural changes may become too dangerous. In previous periods, economic reforms were thought to be desirable, but events proved they were not mandatory. To some extent this was because there was still some margin for maneuver and for error. It now seems that the Soviet Union is simply too close to the edge: in other words, manpower shortages will not disappear, oil will not magically be discovered; hard currency and technology will have to be sought out, foreign debts repaid; etc.

For the West the intriguing question is whether these kinds of pressures on a new leadership will direct attention toward reducing enormous commitments of scarce resources to national defense. The question cannot be answered with any assurance; there are too many political and economic variables, and considerable analysis needs to be done on what the Soviet situation is likely to be in the late 1980s. It needs to be underscored, however, that for the past thirty-five years the Soviet Union, with only a brief interlude, has had a steady commitment to military power. It would take a leader of extraordinary strength and foresight to change this strategic direction. And such a decision would probably flow less from the realities of the Soviet economy than from the costs and benefits of the foreign policy being conducted at the particular time.

## Soviet-American Relations

The Soviet Union enters the 1980s in the strongest position in its history. Never has Soviet power been greater vis-à-vis its principal adversary, the U.S. And never has the ability of the U.S. been weaker in terms of the critical areas of conflict, particularly in the Middle East, the Persian Gulf, and the Indian Ocean. It seems more and more likely that this general area will become the focal point of intense competition and potential conflict.

Ironically, it may be that the course of Soviet-American relations will be determined by events beyond the control of either side—namely, by the situation in Poland. There the Soviet Union faces a fundamental challenge to the Communist system in Eastern Europe. Free institutions, no matter what their guise, cannot co-exist with a totalitarian political system. If the Polish trade unions cannot be circumscribed, then they will have to be crushed by Soviet intervention. If this does in fact happen, the course of Soviet-American relations will be frozen for some years to come, especially if the intervention is bloody; and the budding Soviet-European detente will be undermined if not destroyed. A major trade embargo by the West would seem almost certain, and this would vastly worsen the Soviet internal situation. In this light, Soviet behavior in the Gulf may become extremely dangerous.

The outlook, therefore, is for one of great instability at least through the mid-1980s, until some of the Soviet problems begin to have an impact. Leaving aside Poland, much will depend, of course, on the American response to the Soviet offensive, which seems almost certain to continue until checked by a display of countervailing powers. Indeed, a confrontation in this area between the two superpowers is highly likely.

# The Soviet Union and the Middle East: Another View

## By Robert Legvold

MORE THAN EVER, today's Middle East reaches across two critical regions: the first, the narrow, traditional Near East, dominated by the Arab-Israeli conflict; and the second, a more far-flung area, stretching north, south, and east, dominated by the oil-producing nations and the seaways to them. The two regions have always been interconnected, but, in the past, the first monopolized our attentions and apprehensions. At the moment, the second, focused on the Persian Gulf, is more the preoccupation. In the years ahead, however, both are likely to contribute their fair share to our anxieties. And both are almost certainly going to impinge increasingly on one another. It is this larger, involved, dual context that will shape and be shaped by Soviet foreign policy.

Predicting future Soviet Middle East policy—the rather reckless purpose of these comments—depends in the first instance on how the past is viewed. Disagreements over the Soviet Union's likely course parallel disagreements over what has happened so far. Some think the Soviet leadership has single-mindedly sought to establish its dominance over both halves of the Middle East, using its growing military power to intimidate local elites and West European patrons, exploiting, sometimes instigating, local instability to create opportunities for itself, and struggling against peaceful change and a settlement of the Arab-Israeli conflict for fear of losing out. These persons would expect the Soviet Union to go on in the same way in the future, particularly since Soviet military power is bound to grow and the instability on which it supposedly thrives is probably bound to grow as well.

Others, and I count myself among them, view the picture as more mixed. Soviet policy, though the inspiration of an ambitious and unsatisfied power, has been far from the purposeful and coherent design imagined by many. It has been opportunistic, and at times aggressive and ill-willed toward the West and local regimes the Soviet leadership considers hostile, but it is not the simplistically expansionist, systematic, or relentlessly militant effort implied in much popular analysis. Over the years, the Soviet leadership has shown as much caution as daring in exploiting disorder in the region. It has been as bewildered by the complexity of politics in this region as any other outside leadership. And its policy has been at least as incoherent.

By the same token, neither in fact nor in the Soviet mind have Soviet fortunes been as favored by the general course of events as many in the U.S. seem to feel. The impression that despite setbacks (in Sudan, Somalia, Egypt, among the Islamic nations in the wake of Afghanistan, and so on) the Soviet Union is gaining and the West losing ground is not shared in Moscow. At least not in the simple terms frequently assumed in this country.

True, when the Soviets compare their position in the Middle East at the outset of the new decade with that of the 1970s, the situation must appear more satisfying. From their perspective, the two most salient features of the seventies were the emergence of a quasi-regional security system in the Persian Gulf dominated by an American-befriended Iran and directed against the Soviet Union, and the collapse of the Soviet Union's partnership with Egypt, a loss comparable to the defection of the Yugoslavs in 1948 and the Chinese in the 1960s. Taken together, these two developments made the 1970s the Soviet Union's most frustrating years in the Middle East since it sponsored the Czech sale of arms to Nasser in 1955.

On the eve of the new decade, the Iranian revolution, in an instant, wrecked the notion that a local power might emerge which would be able to aid in stabilizing the region and in checking the spread of Soviet influence. It also devastated the American position in the region, a development openly celebrated in the Soviet press. Whatever else happens, one Soviet commentator would write within weeks of the Shah's fall, never again will U.S. power in the area be the same. In the other part of the Middle East, as the 1980s opened, the consequences of the Soviet estrangement from Egypt had scarcely been reversed (the Soviet Union remained on the physical and political periphery of the region), but its most far-reaching negative effects were partially offset by the stalemate in the Egyptian-Israeli peace process.

Still, from the Soviet vantage point, the direction of events in the Middle East created great uncertainties. A vortex of instability on its southern border, the Gulf region remained as much a worry as an inviting opportunity. American power might have been severely damaged by the passing of the Shah's regime, but the Soviet Union had not gained notably more entree into the area. Politics within and among the Gulf states remained essentially as inaccessible to effective Soviet influence as before. At the same time, the risks inherent in these politics had grown for the Soviet Union. No state, least of all a powerful but uneasy one, likes to see chaos on its borders. The Soviet Union wants weak, not chaotic or fractious, neighbors. When there is trouble, it wants to be able to control it, to step in and sort things out, and above all else to spare itself local crises likely to draw in its major outside competitors.

At the start of the new decade, each of these objectives was as far from the Soviet grasp as it had been in the past. The Soviet Union remained neither a well-regarded peacemaker whose help in pacifying or policing the area appealed to others nearby nor an ally of local states strong enough to bring the Soviets in on their own. And, despite any satisfaction the Soviet leadership took from Western apprehensions over the future of the Gulf, it recognized that any significant upheaval in the area would be likely to bring the United States running with military force. Short of walking away from all military involvement on their own part, a course Soviet leaders were no longer inclined to follow in countries like Afghanistan and probably Iran, this meant that instability in the region now had the most dangerous implications, something apparently appreciated by the Soviet leadership.

On the other side of the Arabian Peninsula, the hazards of instability and the lack of Soviet access, while diminished, were still of concern. The Arab-Israeli conflict remained a cauldron whose brew the Soviet Union could not much affect, since the cooks were elsewhere, but whose fire could burn the Soviet Union if headstrong Soviet clients were careless. Thus, while the Soviet Union had less reason to fear that the Americans and key regional players would work things out to its disadvantage, nothing on the horizon portended a safe way for the Soviet Union to maneuver its way back to a central role. This, it seems to me, is roughly the right perspective from which to begin discussing the future, not least because I think it comes closer to the perspective the Soviets bring to the future.

In my view, the Soviet Union's broad and basic objectives in the Near East have endured for some time and are likely to endure in the future. They include the desire (1) to maximize the Soviet presence and role in the region, preferably by maximizing its presence and role in the key countries of the region; (2) to build the infrastructure of Soviet military power in the region (i.e., to acquire air and naval facilities and to preposition materiel); (3) to shrink the reach as well as the weight of U.S. and allied power in the region; (4) to enhance Soviet influence over the regimes, resources, and access routes that matter to the major Western powers; (5) to foster the political and social transformation of countries in the region; and (6) to promote stability in the region, short of critically jeopardizing any of the other five objectives.[1]

Most of these objectives are related functionally rather than hierarchically (that is, they depend on one another rather than separating into a distinct order of priority); they are reinforcing rather than competing, as the Soviets see things (the Soviets, for example, have always regarded progress toward socialism in the Arab states as something that supports Soviet influence in the area and vice versa); and they retain roughly the same salience, even as new objectives (such as building a regional military infrastructure in post-1967) are added. However, they tell us very little about the nature of Soviet policy in the area or its evolution.

In my view, the Soviet Union's preferred outcome in the Arab-Israeli conflict is also reasonably well-formed, and it, too, has remained relatively constant over the last decade. I do not think it will change in the forseeable future. This preferred outcome, in my judgment, has as its essence a settlement of the Arab-Israeli conflict, provided the Soviet Union is one of its architects and possibly one of its guarantors. While some of the elements in this "settlement" are more uncertain and elastic than others, they include: (1) an acceptance of and guarantee to the state of Israel within its June 4, 1967 borders; (2) the formation of a Palestinian state alongside, not instead of, Israel; (3) a Palestinian state that may but need not be independent of Jordan; (4) a Palestinian state that may but need not—indeed, preferably would not—be dominated by the PLO; (5) the transfer of East Jerusalem to Palestinian authority or alternatively its internationalization; and (6) the right of refugees to return to Israel as circumscribed by U.N. Resolution 194 (those willing "to live in peace with their neighbors"). However, again, this preferred outcome tells us little about the substance of Soviet policy in the Middle East. The path that policy travels and the hazards, impediments, and detours that it encounters en route count for much more than its original intention.

Not that underlying Soviet objectives are irrelevant or inconsequential. However, Soviet actions in the Middle East have much greater importance for Western policy than their objectives, and have more to do with the state of politics within the region. Basic Soviet objectives serve as the parameters of policy; available options serve as its guide and impetus. In the past, the Soviets have not had it within their grasp to displace U.S. power or take Western strategic interests hostage, except in their capacity

1. This qualification, in Soviet eyes, does not make automatic nonsense of the Soviet interest in stability.

to induce a speedy settlement of the Arab-Israeli conflict. This is not likely to change in the near future.

Understanding the actual course of Soviet policy means looking at it where it has been least constant and most contradictory: in its strategy, the decisive dimension of policy now and in the future. Over the past twenty-five years, Soviet Middle Eastern policy has passed through many phases. At each stage important components have changed or added, but the basic divide in the Soviet Union's strategic position in the region— and therefore in its strategy (not the other way around)—has come out but once: in 1975–76.

Before 1975, the heart of Soviet strategy (and the key to its strategic position) was the relationship with Egypt; after 1976 it was living with the collapse of that relationship.[2] For two decades the Soviet approach to the Middle East had been oriented around an effective, if at times vexed, partnership with the Egyptians. The partnership dictated Soviet strategy in the Arab-Israeli conflict, dominated the Soviet response to pan-Arab unity, inspired Soviet hopes for political and social change in the countries of the area, and extended Soviet involvement in local turmoil (such as the Yemen war, 1962–68).

The partnership put the Soviet Union at the center of politics within the region, allied with central players, and on an equal footing with the other superpower. When it disintegrated, each of these critical corollaries collapsed as well. As a result, the Soviet Union was relegated to the physical and political periphery of the region, shut out of three of the key countries (Egypt, Saudi Arabia, and Israel), left in an ambiguous position in the fourth (Iraq), and forced to cede the dominant diplomatic position to the U.S. Whether it liked it or not, its practical choice came down to cultivating the most militant and least influential Arab states (while trying to hold together its shaky position in Syria), and that also meant cultivating the Palestinian issue and, to a lesser extent, the PLO.

Few in Moscow can be delighted with the options this leaves open to Soviet policy. They are left tied to clients with whose substantive position they disagree (and the clients know this), but compelled to act on their behalf, because these states (and the PLO) remain the Soviet Union's sole means of access to the politics of the region. Soviet leaders have seized on their patronage of militant rejectionists and the PLO as their only cur-

2. Though the Soviet-Egyptian relationship was deeply troubled from 1972 on, and moribund after the 1973 war, and though the Soviet leadership had begun by 1974 to develop fragments of what would become an alternative strategy, until the break the Soviet leadership still seemed to operate within the old framework.

rency in the current situation, but, in the process, have made themselves hostage to the stance taken by their clients. All of this, for the moment, is addressed to the lowly mission of restoring the Soviet Union's diplomatic position in the Middle East, a new and unexpected preliminary that must be dealt with before the Soviet leadership can even begin to think about its more substantial objectives.

The Soviet consolation, in the short run, can only be that the post-March 1979 stalemate spares it the need to grapple with the inherent dilemmas of its present strategy; its source of hope, in the longer run, must be that the future of any Arab regime, including the most hostile to the Soviet Union, always remains uncertain and so, too, the course of Middle Eastern events. Here the Soviets have a comparative advantage over the Americans: they have reason to trust uncertainty while we, in the nature of things, must mistrust it.

In the near term, predicting the evolution of Soviet policy in the area is hazardous because it depends so heavily on the evolution of the Middle East context. Several parts of the equation, however, can be anticipated. *First*, the Soviet Union has several intermediate objectives to which it is likely to apply itself with energy, given half a chance. One is to pick up the small change—providing succor and attention to any disaffected party that might be drawn away from the moderate Arab or Western side, working in the cracks of the region's international system. The second is to prejudice Egyptian foreign policy at every turn, and, better yet, to work at undermining Sadat himself. The third is to keep up a drumbeat of opposition to the Camp David process and to encourage separate initiatives that might detract from it, including those of the West Europeans. The fourth is to hedge Soviet bets, reaching out as much as possible to the Jordanians and Saudis while doing no less with radical elements in the PLO and other quarters; however, this does not mean to gamble or to make alliance reversals or dramatic choices say, for example, between Syria and Iraq or, in a broader setting, between Iran and Iraq.

*Second*, if the Camp David process goes forward, producing the first solid outlines of a settlement different from the one preferred by the Soviet Union, the Soviet Union is likely to run considerable risks in supporting countries and collaborators willing to sabotage it. If the Camp David process goes forward, but without prejudicing the settlement the Soviet Union seeks or without threatening to lock the Soviet Union out for another half decade or longer, the Soviet Union is likely to play the role of a restrained spoiler. If the Camp David process is stalemated, the Soviet Union is likely to invigorate its diplomacy, trying a variety of political initiatives. What these might entail will depend entirely on changing leaderships, alignments, and frictions within the region. If the Camp David process collapses, the Soviet Union is likely to moderate its superficially hard line on the issues in hopes of getting a larger negotiation under way. If the collapse of the Camp David process accompanies the passing of the Begin government, the Soviet leadership may go about this by distancing itself from its current radical clients and conciliating the Israelis. In the interstices of these various futures, if the present stalemate gives way to a Jordanian option, enjoying the support of the Saudis and other moderates, the Soviets may turn out to be surprisingly tolerant—provided a way can be found to link this stage with a responsible and meaningful role for the Soviet Union the next time around.

*Third*, how troublesome, impatient, or destructive the Soviet Union is in the Arab-Israeli conflict is in some degree a function of the state of U.S.-Soviet relations. The least auspicious aspect of each of the above scenarios will emerge if the relationship remains angry and conflict-ridden. Each will be most benign if tensions between the two ease and some level of cooperation is restored. Thus, predicting things to come in the U.S.-Soviet relationship is the key to predicting Soviet behavior in the Middle East. Since the larger relationship appears to be staggering into a relatively lengthy interlude of exaggerated mistrust, this is likely to be an unpromising picture. At the same time, it is worth remembering that, as Soviet-American friction in the Middle East has been both cause and effect in the general deterioration of Soviet-American relations, so a more constructive interaction in the Middle East can be both cause and effect in an improving relationship.

In the wake of the Iranian revolution and the invasion of Afghanistan, the link between developments in the inner and outer regions of the Middle East seems certain to be reinforced. Oil will ensure that the apprehensions and actions of key outsiders see to it. The Arabian Peninsula, now the bridge between these two critical theaters, will ensure that instability anywhere from Aden to Kuwait City reverberates in either direction. And, if the current war between Iraq and Iran is any indication, conflicts in one region will agitate, complicate, and sometimes transform alignments and tensions in the other. Each part of the Middle East may increasingly import the international politics of the other.

By and large the Soviet Union has not been shrewd in anticipating this coupling or interpretation of the region's two parts. It no has particular stakes in it, nor has it designed policy to affect it one way or another. Oil, in my view, does not serve as an impetus to Soviet policymakers. I doubt that oil, either as a commodity to deny an energy-dependent West or to grab for an energy-depleted East, will play more than a marginal role in shaping Soviet policy toward the region over the next five years. The popular nightmare of a Soviet Union with oil fields suddenly gone dry coveting and then leaning on the West's Persian Gulf supply seems far-fetched. The Soviets have problems ahead, something they know and are now belatedly but energetically addressing. Almost certainly by the mid-1980s they will not be able to squeeze from oil and gas exports the same rate of hard currency earning, while supplying the East Europeans and their own economy the same increments of fuel as in the past. However, the notion that the overall shortfall will be great enough to inspire desperate acts—and tampering with the flow of OPEC-controlled Arab oil would be an act of desperation—stretches the problem out of proportion. The Soviet Union will have a mounting commercial, not colonial, interest in Persian Gulf oil and gas in the current decade.[3] This interest will not be expressed in the gangster's way of doing commerce—that is, not by extortion—nor by the equivalent of "selling protection." The Soviets will be looking for more opportunities like IGAT I and II, including the restoration of IGAT I and a start on IGAT II, and more such as the arrangements the East Europeans have begun working out with the Iraqis. These opportunities are not going to be generated by the ham-handed use of military power. They are not even going to be aided by instability and disorder in the area. On the contrary. That is not lost on Moscow.

Neither, in my view, does the Soviet response to the intertwining of events in the Near East and the Gulf derive an inner order from the development of a more ambitious or militant strategy in the Third World. I do not believe the Soviet Union has consciously launched a major offensive in the Persian Gulf region, any more than I believe that the Soviet Union has launched a conscious, even loosely coordinated, offensive in the Third World of which Soviet probing in the Persian Gulf region is a part. Soviet adventures from Angola to Afghanistan do represent important departures in Soviet behavior, but not yet a policy pattern. Even less, in my judgment, do they reflect the working out of some clear concept of what opportunities are to be seized, toward what end, or by what application of military power. There is not a systematic design, nor a calculated decision to forge a "new alliance system" in the Third World, nor a determination to bring the "Brezhnev doctrine" to Third World revolution-making.

There is a new assertiveness in Soviet policy, a heightening of traditional opportunism, and a readiness to use military power in places and

3. These terms are Shahram's Chubin's in "Soviet Policy towards Iran and the Gulf," *Adelphi Papers*, no. 157 (Spring 1980), pp. 9–10.

ways never tried before. Earlier, when arguing that oil was not likely to make the Soviet Union more of a military problem in the Persian Gulf region, I was not saying that the Soviet Union was not or would not become more of a military problem. As Afghanistan dramatically demonstrates, the Soviet Union is prepared to use military force in the region. In Afghanistan it rather lightheartedly embraced impetuous conspirators, who then slid into deep trouble, leaving a less-than-discerning Soviet leadership to bail them out with the one tool the Soviet Union has in abundance. In general, the Soviets do appear increasingly surly with regard to the forms of instability and freedom of U.S. action they are willing to tolerate in the region. However, this scarcely adds up to the kind of self-conscious policy which would prompt the Soviet leadership to think grand thoughts about the Persian Gulf region as a whole or to develop ambitious and well-integrated strategies. The Iraqi-Iranian war is doubtless teaching Soviet leaders about the complicated ways the politics of the two regions are likely to intermix and about the need to take this new factor into account in designing policy. However, the Soviet Union has not and will not soon, in my judgment, develop a grand strategy by which they act in the greater Middle East.

Indeed, Soviet policy, as is the case with our own, remains captive to unforeseeable events that often remake the political landscape. No Soviet policymaker could have been prescient enough to anticipate the chain of events that terminated in a threat to the Soviet Union's key relationship with Iraq, a chain of events apparently much influenced by changes in Iran. The Iraqis appear to have gone to war with Iran in answer to Khomeini's subversive appeal to Shi'ite Arabs, a majority of Iraq's people, and encouraged by the Iranian weaknesses obvious in the wake of its revolution. The inter-Arab politics of the war have made the Iraqis more dependent on the moderate states, and have reinforced Saddam Hussein's recent inclination to distance Iraq from its Soviet benefactors. If the transformation of Arab alignments, accentuated by the war, continues, the field in which Soviet policy must operate will once more have been dramatically altered.

If only the politics of the Middle East changed in a regular pattern or, at a minimum, by simple, stark turns, the Soviet leadership might think it possible to devise a relatively comprehensive and settled strategy. The trouble is the patterns are not regular, and change is not like a pendulum, it is like a kaleidoscope.

In the absence of a systematic Soviet approach to the Third World, or even to the targets of opportunity created by instability, Soviet actions in Africa and South Asia do not have the menacing bearing on Soviet policy in the Middle East that is sometimes argued. There are intrinsic reasons to be concerned about the course of Soviet policy in each of these other regions, but not a transcendent geostrategic one as sometimes too casually asserted.

However, one need not believe the Soviet Union has launched a major "geostrategic offensive," or has entered a new "imperial phase" in its development, or has in place an integrated strategy, to recognize that Soviet policy in the Gulf region poses a grave challenge, and that the period ahead in this area of the world holds great danger. Given the simultaneous increase in Soviet assertiveness and insecurity, paralleled by something similar on the American side, the process by which great, but disturbed, powers lose control seems more likely to accelerate in the Middle East than any place else. In the Gulf region itself, the most hazardous case is Iran (and beyond the Gulf, in my judgment, it is Pakistan). In Iran, in the context of a disintegrating regime or nation-state, the two countries are capable of getting themselves into enormous trouble.

Avoiding a direct military confrontation with the Soviet Union, while at the same time inducing or compelling Soviet restraint on the northern approaches to the Persian Gulf, will require more political skill than we may possess in coming years. To be effective, U.S. policymakers will not only have to know how to draw the line and make it credible by marshalling the necessary military resources, but also will have to know how to reach out to the Soviet Union and engage its leadership in a more constructive effort at crisis management in this explosive area. To deal with the Soviet challenge in the Persian Gulf by developing only one of these two policy elements invites tragedy. Because the risks of U.S.-Soviet conflict in the Persian Gulf are of a different magnitude from those of conflict in the Near East, so is the importance of a carefully balanced U.S. policy there. In neither part of the Middle East can the United States afford a weak policy, but in the Persian Gulf it cannot afford only a militarily strong policy.

# Part II:
# Economic and Social Determinants
# of Stability

# Oil Prices and the World Economy

## By Lawrence R. Klein

WHEN OIL PRICES first began to escalate, in late 1973, economists made many hurried estimates under pressure of circumstances and produced a wide range of results. Some saw the problems as temporary, some as self-rectifying, and some as overwhelming. Now that "the dust has settled" and analysts have been able to build more energy content into quantitative economic analysis, we are able to draw a more assured view of the economic consequences of scarce energy resources. A consensus has developed along many lines. The issues are more widely and more deeply understood. There is not perfect agreement (there hardly ever is such a thing among economists), but the kinds of results and conjectures that I shall put forward in this paper should not be surprising.

Even before 1973, operators of the Wharton Models wrestled with the problems looming for the American economy as a result of rising oil imports. Taking heed of warnings given us by the economists from oil companies participating in the forecast operations of Wharton Econometric Forecasting Associates, we factored in a strongly rising volume of oil imports over the 1970s and 1980s. The need for imports arose because of the shortfall of domestic supplies. The trouble with these older projections was that tiny price increases were estimated. They were so small that I dare not say what they amounted to, quantitatively. Nevertheless, the rising volume of projected imports unsettled the external accounts of the United States and induced a slower trend growth rate. If the economy were stimulated for faster growth, more energy imports were needed and this worsened the balance of payments position, requiring adverse adjustment elsewhere in the economy.

The physical embargo of 1973–74 exerted a predictable effect on the economy; it generated a recession. We model builders were unprepared for the enormous surge in oil prices and underestimated inflationary pressures for the remainder of the decade of the 1970s. At the present time, however, we have absorbed the price transmission mechanism and have come to some conclusions with regard to the impact of energy prices on

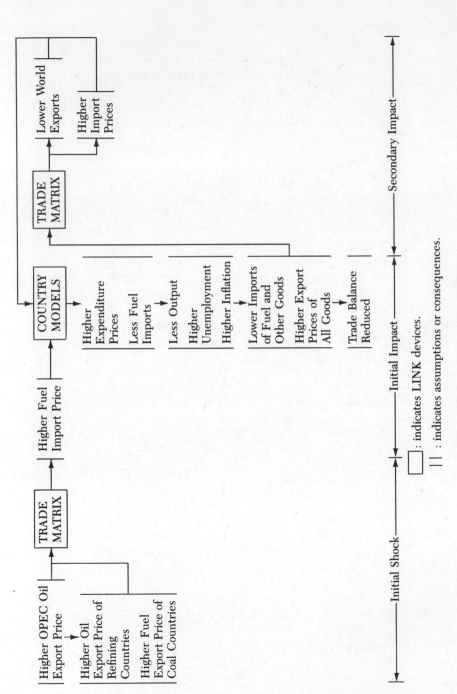

**Fig. 1. The flow chart of the effect of an OPEC price increase in the LINK system**

domestic prices, not only for the United States but for the whole community of oil importing industrial countries. As for energy exporters such as the U.K., Canada, Norway, and a few others, we have some slightly different results that appear to be plausible in light of the different circumstances of these countries.

The box-flow diagram in Fig. 1 shows how oil prices work their way through the economy, affecting overall domestic prices, trade accounts, output levels, employment, and related magnitudes. Even though energy expenses are a tiny fraction of the total GDP, price increases of energy products result in highly discernible increases in the overall inflation rate.

First, consider a major oil importing country by itself. This brings us to the third segment, from the left, in the diagram. Higher fuel import prices lead to markups of domestic prices in lines that rely significantly on fuel inputs or on petroleum based feed stocks. Basically, prices in the Western industrial countries are formed by marking up unit costs and fuel costs are among these, others being labor, materials and capital. Increases in fuel efficiency can offset the rise in unit fuel costs, but such efficiencies take time to realize and are limited. However, they do help and have figured importantly in relieving some inflationary tensions in recent years.

The high price of fuel imports discourages consumption of fuel and less is consumed. The lower input of fuel leads initially to lower total output, until an adjustment can be made for fuel substitution or conservation. This adjustment takes time.

Higher overall prices, based on cost markup, means more inflation and a general reduction of physical consumption of goods. As export prices rise, in line with domestic prices, the ability to sell goods abroad is reduced. The trade balance worsens on the export side because of price increases and on the import side because of high fuel import costs. A deteriorating balance on external account induces currency depreciation and higher import costs all round. This sparks another round of price markups.

When this chain of events happens to several importing countries all at once, they import less, overall, because activity falls or grows more slowly and import prices rise. If major importers are cut back, then exporters to them will also lose international sales. This amplifies the effect on a world scale. World trade falls below its normal expansion path. This hits, especially, the developing countries who need a strong volume of world trade to maintain their own export volumes. They, in effect, have a "share" of world trade.

The oil exporting countries in the industrial world (the U.K. and Norway, in particular) experience inflation because their internal energy prices follow world energy prices closely. Also, there is a pressure of demand as a result of boom conditions in the oil producing areas. They do not have balance of payments troubles and pressures for currency depreciation. This sets them apart from other Western industrial nations.

OPEC nations are beneficiaries of the high prices, even if it means a reduced volume of oil production. Their total GDP may be held in restraint because petroleum volume is restrained, but their nominal receipts are comfortably large and they have large purchasing power throughout the world. If we deflated their nominal income by prices of things that OPEC nations buy—durables and other goods produced and exported by industrial countries—we would find, in the main, that they gained significantly.

Another way of looking at OPEC countries is through the medium of their non oil sectors. This is where their growth and development efforts are focussed. Regardless of oil volume, the non oil sectors are well financed and on the way to completion. Apart from the usual inflationary pressures that are felt almost everywhere in the world, conditions in the oil exporting countries look favorable overall. Notable among oil exporters pursuing large nonoil development programs is Mexico, but it is not an OPEC member.

The OPEC countries, particularly those on the Persian Gulf, have all the growing pains of rapid economic development. In addition, they have an explosive domestic situation as a result of heavy reliance on imported labor. In some Middle East economies, 50 percent or more of the labor force comes from abroad—from Korea, India, Pakistan, Thailand, etc.

The higher prices at the right of Fig. 1 go back into the world trade system and enter the world economy again through an induced round of price increases—higher import prices into each country and export prices from it.

The most visible international manifestation of trade and payments problems stemming from energy pricing is the existence of a large OPEC current account surplus. In a total system where the world sum of current account balances is zero, the OPEC surplus should be matched by deficits elsewhere. In spite of the fact that reported current account balances do not sum to zero over all countries together, the main effect shows through in the form of an OPEC surplus and an OECD deficit.

The economic consequences of the OPEC surplus is that it gets invested round the world in asset holdings, many of them in debt or equity instruments in the main industrial countries. Apart from political and industrial organization effects, the associated international movements of capital have significant impact on exchange rates, particularly on the U.S.

## Table 1

### Effects of Oil Price Changes
### Changes in World Totals

| | 1979 | 1980 | 1981 | 1982 | 1983 | 1984 | 1985 |
|---|---|---|---|---|---|---|---|
| | | | *(in billions of U.S. dollars)* | | | | |
| **Trade Balances** | | | | | | | |
| OECD | −15.6 | −23.6 | −38.9 | −55.4 | −74.2 | −98.0 | −124.5 |
| Developed | | | | | | | |
| Countries | 13.4 | 20.7 | 35.3 | 50.8 | 68.9 | 91.3 | 117.4 |
| CMEA | 1.9 | 2.4 | 3.4 | 4.8 | 5.9 | 7.6 | 9.0 |
| Rest of World | 0.3 | 0.4 | 0.1 | − 0.2 | − 0.5 | − 1.0 | − 1.9 |
| | | | *(percentages)* | | | | |
| World export price | 1.8 | 0.9 | 1.7 | 1.3 | 1.5 | 1.2 | 1.5 |
| Volume world | | | | | | | |
| exports | − 1.5 | − 0.7 | − 0.6 | − 0.9 | − 0.7 | − 0.2 | − 0.3 |
| World oil export | | | | | | | |
| price | 8.5 | 3.2 | 6.5 | 5.2 | 4.6 | 5.2 | 4.8 |
| GDP (LINK-OECD) | − 0.5 | − 0.4 | − 0.5 | − 0.4 | − 0.4 | − 0.4 | − 0.4 |
| Consumer price | | | | | | | |
| deflator | 0.3 | 0.3 | 0.5 | 0.4 | 0.4 | 0.4 | 0.4 |

dollar, which is the present unit of denomination for oil prices. To some extent a cumulative process develops. Oil exporting countries accumulate a balance-of-payments surplus. This can be invested in ways that push down the values of certain currencies like the dollar. As the dollar sinks, OPEC tries for higher prices to compensate for its loss of purchasing power. This increases its surplus further and causes another round of dollar depreciation. To some extent there are offsets because dollar denominated exports in general become more attractive and imports become dearer for the U.S., leading to some marginal improvement in trade accounts.

It is a complicated process, from the side of trade, payments, exchange rates, and domestic activity all over the world. How does it all work out? A typical pair of world scenarios from project LINK are compared in Table 1. A base case is compared in Table 1 with a scenario in which world export prices for oil are higher than the base by 8.5 percentage points in 1979 and about 5 percentage points, 1980–85.

The higher world oil prices lower the industrial world GDP growth rate and raise the inflation rate. The OECD growth rate is set back by about 0.4 percent for the whole period. The increase in the inflation rate also

**Table 2**

Individual Country Results of Oil—A Simulation,
The Growth Rate of GNP

| Country | 1979 Pre | 1979 Post | 1980 Pre | 1980 Post | 1981 Pre | 1981 Post | 1982 Pre | 1982 Post | 1983 Pre | 1983 Post | 1984 Pre | 1984 Post | 1985 Pre | 1985 Post |
|---|---|---|---|---|---|---|---|---|---|---|---|---|---|---|
| Australia | 0 | -.1 | 0 | -.1 | 0 | -.1 | 0 | 0 | 0 | 0 | 0 | 0 | 0 | 0 |
| Austria | .1 | -.3 | .1 | 0 | 0 | 0 | 0 | 0 | 0 | .1 | 0 | 0 | 0 | 0 |
| Belgium | .4 | -.5 | -.2 | -.3 | .2 | -.3 | 0 | -.3 | -.1 | -.3 | .1 | -.1 | 0 | -.1 |
| Canada | 0 | 0 | 0 | .1 | 0 | -.1 | 0 | 0.3 | 0 | 0.3 | 0 | 0.3 | 0 | .2 |
| Finland | -.2 | -.4 | .1 | -.4 | .1 | -.3 | .1 | -.2 | .1 | -.2 | 0 | -.1 | 0 | -.1 |
| France | -.2 | -.5 | .1 | -.4 | 0.1 | -.4 | .1 | -.4 | .1 | -.4 | 0 | -.4 | 0 | -.4 |
| Germany | 0.8 | -.8 | .2 | -.2 | -.4 | -.8 | 0 | -.7 | .1 | -.7 | .1 | -.6 | 0 | -.5 |
| Italy | -.3 | -.7 | -.2 | -.5 | -.1 | -.8 | 0 | -.6 | 0 | -.7 | 0 | -.6 | 0 | -.7 |
| Japan | -.3 | -.4 | 0 | -.3 | 0 | -.3 | 0 | -.2 | 0 | -.3 | 0 | -.2 | 0 | -.4 |
| Netherlands | | 1.0 | | -.2 | | -.8 | | -1.2 | | -1.2 | | -1.2 | | -1.0 |
| Sweden | -.1 | -.4 | 0 | -.3 | -.1 | -.3 | -.1 | -.4 | -.1 | -.5 | 0 | -.5 | 0 | -.5 |
| U.K. | -.1 | -.4 | .1 | -.2 | 0 | -.3 | 0 | -.2 | 0 | -.2 | 0 | -.3 | 0 | -.3 |
| U.S. | -.3 | -.5 | .1 | -.5 | -.1 | -.7 | 0 | -.5 | 0 | -.4 | .1 | -.4 | .1 | -.5 |

## Table 3

### Individual Country Results of Oil—A Simulation, The Inflation Rate of CPI

| Country | 1979 Pre | 1979 Post | 1980 Pre | 1980 Post | 1981 Pre | 1981 Post | 1982 Pre | 1982 Post | 1983 Pre | 1983 Post | 1984 Pre | 1984 Post | 1985 Pre | 1985 Post |
|---|---|---|---|---|---|---|---|---|---|---|---|---|---|---|
| Australia | 0 | .1 | 0 | .1 | 0 | .1 | 0 | .2 | 0 | .2 | 0 | .2 | 0 | .3 |
| Austria | 0 | .1 | 0 | 0 | 0 | 0 | 0 | .1 | 0 | .1 | 0 | .1 | 0 | .1 |
| Belgium | .2 | .2 | 0 | .3 | 0 | .4 | .1 | .4 | 0 | .4 | .1 | .4 | 0 | .4 |
| Canada | .4 | .3 | −.1 | .5 | .2 | .5 | 0 | .8 | −.1 | .8 | 0 | 1.0 | 0 | 1.0 |
| Finland | 0 | .1 | 0 | .1 | 0 | .1 | 0 | .2 | −.1 | .1 | −.1 | .1 | 0 | .1 |
| France | 1.1 | 1.2 | −.6 | .7 | .5 | 1.1 | 0 | 1.0 | −.1 | 1.0 | −.1 | 1.2 | 0 | 1.2 |
| Germany | | | | | | | | | | | | | | |
| Italy | .4 | .4 | .1 | .5 | .1 | .6 | .1 | .6 | 0 | .7 | 0 | .7 | −.1 | .7 |
| Japan | .3 | .2 | −.1 | .2 | 0 | .3 | 0 | .2 | −.1 | .1 | 0 | .1 | 0 | .1 |
| Netherlands | | .1 | | .3 | | .7 | | .9 | | .9 | | .7 | | .5 |
| Sweden | .2 | .1 | 0 | .1 | .1 | .3 | .1 | .3 | 0 | .4 | .1 | .4 | 0 | .3 |
| U.K. | .4 | .4 | −.1 | .4 | −.1 | .7 | 0 | .9 | 0 | 1.0 | 0 | 1.0 | 0 | .9 |
| U.S. | .3 | .3 | −.1 | .3 | .1 | .5 | 0 | .4 | −.1 | .3 | −.1 | .3 | 0 | .4 |

**Table 4**

Individual Country Results of Oil—A Simulation,
The Inflation Rate of PGNP

| Country | 1979 Pre | 1979 Post | 1980 Pre | 1980 Post | 1981 Pre | 1981 Post | 1982 Pre | 1982 Post | 1983 Pre | 1983 Post | 1984 Pre | 1984 Post | 1985 Pre | 1985 Post |
|---|---|---|---|---|---|---|---|---|---|---|---|---|---|---|
| Australia | -.2 | -.1 | .1 | .1 | 0 | .1 | 0 | .2 | 0 | .2 | 0 | .2 | 0 | .3 |
| Austria | 0 | .1 | 0 | -.1 | 0 | -.1 | 0 | -.1 | 0 | -.1 | 0 | 0 | 0 | 0 |
| Belgium | 0 | .2 | .4 | .4 | -.1 | .2 | .2 | .3 | .1 | .3 | 0 | .3 | .1 | .2 |
| Canada | .1 | .3 | 0 | .4 | .1 | .7 | 0 | .7 | -.1 | .7 | 0 | .8 | 0 | .8 |
| Finland | .1 | .2 | -.1 | .1 | -.1 | 0 | -.1 | -.1 | -.1 | -.2 | -.1 | -.2 | 0 | -.2 |
| France | .7 | .8 | .4 | .6 | .2 | .8 | 0 | .8 | -.1 | .8 | 0 | 1.0 | 0 | .9 |
| Germany | -.2 | -.3 | .1 | -.2 | -.2 | -.4 | -.1 | -.5 | 0 | -.4 | -.1 | -.5 | 0 | -.5 |
| Italy | -.1 | .1 | .7 | .4 | -.1 | .3 | .1 | .3 | .1 | .5 | 0.0 | .4 | 0 | .5 |
| Japan | 0.1 | .1 | 0 | .1 | 0 | .1 | 0 | .1 | 0 | -.1 | 0 | -.2 | 0 | -.1 |
| Netherlands | | .1 | | .2 | | .4 | | .6 | | .6 | | .5 | | .4 |
| Sweden | -.1 | -.1 | .2 | 0 | -.1 | -.1 | .1 | .1 | .1 | .1 | 0 | 0 | 0 | -.1 |
| U.K. | .2 | .1 | 0 | .3 | 0 | .6 | 0 | .7 | 0 | .7 | 0 | .6 | 0 | .7 |
| U.S. | 0 | 0 | 0 | .1 | 0 | .2 | 0 | .2 | 0 | .1 | 0 | .1 | 0 | .1 |

**Table 5**

Individual Country Results of Oil—A Simulation,
The Unemployment Rate

| Country | 1979 Pre | 1979 Post | 1980 Pre | 1980 Post | 1981 Pre | 1981 Post | 1982 Pre | 1982 Post | 1983 Pre | 1983 Post | 1984 Pre | 1984 Post | 1985 Pre | 1985 Post |
|---|---|---|---|---|---|---|---|---|---|---|---|---|---|---|
| Australia | 0 | .02 | 0 | .05 | 0 | .08 | 0 | .10 | 0 | .14 | 0 | .19 | 0 | .25 |
| Austria | | | | | | | | | | | | | | |
| Belgium | 0 | .04 | 0 | .10 | 0 | .13 | 0 | .16 | 0 | .16 | 0 | .16 | 0 | .13 |
| Canada | 0 | .06 | 0 | .09 | .1 | .17 | .1 | .15 | 0 | .08 | .1 | .0 | 0 | −.06 |
| Finland | 0.04 | .07 | .07 | .18 | .08 | .27 | .10 | .33 | .10 | .38 | .10 | .40 | .12 | .42 |
| France | | | | | | | | | | | | | | |
| Germany | .15 | .2 | .14 | .4 | .17 | .6 | .2 | .8 | .13 | 1.1 | .11 | 1.4 | | 1.5 |
| Italy | .03 | .13 | .13 | .34 | .20 | .61 | .24 | .90 | .26 | 1.25 | .26 | 1.50 | .26 | 1.92 |
| Japan | .01 | 0 | .03 | .04 | .02 | .08 | .02 | 0.10 | .01 | .10 | 0 | .09 | 0 | .08 |
| Netherlands | | .2 | | .1 | | .3 | | .6 | | .9 | | 1.2 | | 1.5 |
| Sweden | .02 | .11 | .04 | .23 | .06 | .33 | .08 | .42 | .1 | .55 | .11 | .70 | .12 | .87 |
| U.K. | .02 | .08 | .02 | .19 | .02 | .30 | .02 | .42 | .01 | .52 | .01 | .61 | .02 | .72 |
| U.S. | .08 | .13 | .09 | .31 | .10 | .54 | .12 | .78 | .12 | .97 | .11 | 1.18 | .09 | 1.48 |

**Table 6**

Individual Country Results of Oil—A Simulation,
The Trade Balance (*in current billion dollars*)

| Country | 1979 Pre | 1979 Post | 1980 Pre | 1980 Post | 1981 Pre | 1981 Post | 1982 Pre | 1982 Post | 1983 Pre | 1983 Post | 1984 Pre | 1984 Post | 1985 Pre | 1985 Post |
|---|---|---|---|---|---|---|---|---|---|---|---|---|---|---|
| Australia | -.13 | -.13 | -.04 | -.18 | -.12 | -.18 | -.13 | -.16 | -.11 | -.08 | -.15 | .04 | -.13 | .04 |
| Austria | -.02 | -.10 | .01 | -.10 | -.01 | -.15 | .0 | -.20 | 0 | -.23 | 0 | -.27 | 0 | .30 |
| Belgium | .93 | -.29 | .30 | -.48 | .74 | -.76 | .75 | -1.13 | .65 | -1.46 | .84 | -1.90 | .63 | -2.37 |
| Canada | -.43 | 0 | .20 | -.1 | -.43 | .31 | -.47 | .73 | -.43 | 1.16 | -.52 | 1.58 | -.45 | 1.64 |
| Finland | -.02 | -.12 | .01 | -.15 | -.01 | -.24 | -.02 | -.37 | -.02 | -.52 | -.03 | -.73 | -.04 | -.94 |
| France | -.74 | -1.12 | -.16 | -1.62 | -.79 | -2.69 | -.69 | -3.75 | -.70 | -4.93 | -.97 | -6.31 | -.87 | -8.27 |
| Germany | -1.3 | -1.8 | -.23 | -2.3 | -.58 | -2.9 | -.57 | -3.5 | -.25 | -4.3 | -.57 | -5.4 | -.53 | -7.3 |
| Italy | -.93 | -.9 | .17 | -1.1 | -.43 | -1.6 | -.35 | -2.2 | .08 | -2.7 | -.29 | -3.5 | -.03 | -4.6 |
| Japan | -2.85 | -4.5 | -1.03 | -6.7 | -3.14 | -11.2 | -3.54 | -16.4 | -3.31 | -22.8 | -4.5 | -31.0 | -4.03 | -42.1 |
| Netherlands |  | -.3 |  | -.6 |  | -.8 |  | -.5 |  | -.04 |  | .38 |  | .99 |
| Sweden | -.16 | -.36 | 0 | -.52 | -.21 | -.91 | -.21 | -1.41 | -.20 | -2.0 | -.29 | -2.66 | -.26 | -3.64 |
| U.K. | .37 | -.36 | .41 | -.38 | .56 | -.51 | .66 | -.73 | .70 | -.75 | .91 | -.73 | .93 | -.64 |
| U.S. | -2.95 | -5.55 | -.34 | -9.2 | -3.18 | -17.6 | -3.81 | -26.4 | -3.38 | -36.6 | -4.28 | -49.2 | -3.71 | -64.1 |

averages about 0.4 percent. World trade volume is more seriously hurt. It is set back by growing, on average, by 1 percent less at the beginning of the simulation exercise. This margin is reduced to about 0.2 percent or 0.3 percent near the end of the computer run. The OPEC surplus is reflected in the growing trade balance for developing countries, including oil importers and exporters. The corresponding OECD trade deficit is also plainly visible.

# OPEC's Pricing Policy and Its Limits

## BY JOHN H. LICHTBLAU

PROFESSOR KLEIN'S PAPER demonstrates clearly and neatly the negative effect of world oil price increases on the economies of the OECD countries. The paper also illustrates how these price increases create foreign trade surpluses in the oil exporting developing countries. Thus, if world oil prices increase at a faster rate than inflation, economic growth in the industrial countries is slowed down while inflation is accelerated. Hence, an important determinant of economic conditions in the industrial countries over the next five–ten years will be whether world oil prices will rise faster than inflation and, if so, by how much.

Recent history may provide some clue to the answer. Oil prices soared between 1972 and 1974, declined slightly in real terms in the following four years, and increased again very sharply in 1979 and the first quarter of 1980. Altogether, the monetary oil price increase over the last eight years was on the order of 1500 percent, while the real price increase (adjusted for inflation in the industrial countries) was about 700 percent.

Since this monumental price increase was not due to increases in oil production cost, but was collectively decreed and enforced by the members of OPEC, there is a general assumption that without OPEC's function as a price administering organization, world oil prices would be much lower today than they actually are.

The assumption is undoubtedly correct. But it is equally correct to assume that even under the freest of market conditions the *real* price of oil would have risen very rapidly from the mid-1970s on, at the latest. Thus, the era of low-cost oil which played a significant role in shaping the world economy in the first twenty-five years of the postwar period would have come to an end in the 1970s even without OPEC's market intervention. The long-term world oil price of the 1960s and early 1970s had stimulated a long-term world oil demand increase averaging about 7.5 percent annually. Had growth continued at that rate from 1973, or even at a substantially reduced rate (assuming a rapid increase in market saturation during the 1970s), the amount of oil required by 1980 would have been demonstrably more than the physical and technical petroleum resource base would have been able to provide.

Thus, at a growth rate of just 4.5 percent annually, non-Communist world (NCW) oil demand this year would have been 65 million B/D instead of the actual 50 million B/D. If all OPEC members had maintained output at their hypothetical maximum sustainable capacity throughout 1980, they would have been able to supply slightly less than half the difference between these two figures. And, of course, at the oil price assumed for the 4.5 percent demand growth rate (which was nearly six times the actual growth rate registered during this period), non-OPEC oil supplies would have grown by far less than the 3.5 million B/D realized between 1973 and 1980. This would have raised the supply/demand gap still further.

Thus, real prices had to rise sharply during the 1970s, both to curtail demand and to increase supplies. Without OPEC, the rise would probably have started one or two years later and would not have reached such a high level by 1980. If the end-1980 world price had been, say, $23/Bbl instead of the actual $33, it still would have fitted the description of a "sharp rise" (about 36 percent *annually* from 1972 on!). Yet the OECD economies would have been in a significantly better state, as can be calculated from Professor Klein's econometric model.

An indication that the world oil price would have risen more slowly if it had been determined by market forces instead of OPEC edicts lies in the fact that, since 1974, OPEC has had a collective excess producing capacity of substantial proportion in all years but 1979.[1] In a free market this excess capacity would not have occurred or, if it did, would have been reduced through a lowering of prices and a resulting rise in demand. Thus, under OPEC-imposed market conditions, prices were somewhat higher, and demand growth—at a 0.6 percent annual rate—somewhat lower than under free market conditions.

Given the fact that OPEC set prices at a higher level than technical and physical limitations on available supplies would have required, the question is, will or can the organization continue this practice throughout the 1980s and beyond? In answer, we must examine first how OPEC has intervened in the market in the past.

It did so principally by putting a permanent floor under temporary price increases brought about by extraneous short-term events. The first such event was, of course, the Arab oil export embargo of October

1. The impact of the Iranian-Iraqi war on oil supplies is not considered here since it was minimal in 1980, partly because the war started late in that year (end-September) and partly because of exceptionally high oil inventories.

1973–March 1974. The second was the export interruption caused by the Iranian revolution in 1979. In both cases OPEC, through collective action, succeeded in converting part of the market (i.e., spot price increases) caused by the temporary shortage—whether real or perceived—into permanent increases of official government sales prices.

During the four years between these two events OPEC members were unable to prevent some decline in real prices. However, the fact that, in the face of a substantial oil surplus throughout that period, they managed to raise monetary prices at all from the record level attained in 1974 is evidence of successful market intervention by OPEC.

We also know what price increase OPEC had in mind for 1979 under the assumption of adequate supplies, and what the actual OPEC price increases were when supplies turned out to be inadequate. Once more, market forces temporarily drove prices up while OPEC subsequently prevented them from coming down again.

Thus history tells us that in periods of adequate supply, OPEC oil prices tend to register little or no real price increase. Our hope of entering such a period may have been shattered by the outbreak of the Iranian-Iraqi war. The amount of oil exports lost from these two nations, about 4 million B/D, is substantially more than other oil exporters are willing or able to make up. Consequently, higher-than-normal inventory reductions are taking place. Given the high global level of stocks at the beginning of the war, the impact of this inventory reduction will not be felt for a while. But if the war continues for a few more months, and if postwar repairs of damaged oil export installations take several more months, supplies will be tight throughout the first half of 1981. This would lead to market price increases which OPEC members, acting collectively or separately, could once again freeze into higher official sales prices.

However, it may be argued that there must be some real long-term economic ceiling to oil prices—that is, some price above which the producer would eventually sustain a net loss in income, since the increase would be more than offset by a decline in demand.

There have been suggestions that this price may actually have been reached, as evidenced by the decline in oil demand in the OECD area last year, this year, and probably also next year (following an annual growth rate of only 0.5 percent in the previous five years). There is an even more pronounced decline in oil imports into this area which is the destination of 90% of OPEC's exports.

It is not likely that the decline in OECD oil demand will continue at the 1979–81 rate beyond next year. In fact, the direction may well be temporarily reversed after 1981. However, the long-term trend is clearly downward. By 1990, the Western industrial countries' collective oil requirements can be expected to be 3–4 pecent, or about 1.5 million B/D, below the 1980 level. All of the decline will be in the form of reduced imports, which will drop by a larger percentage than demand. In part, this will be a consequence of the introduction of synthetic oil fuels in North America on a commercial scale, as a direct result of the latest OPEC price increase. For this reason, the decline in oil imports may accelerate in the 1990s when synthetic fuels are expected to play a much greater role than in the 1980s.

In the less developed countries (LDC's), oil demand can be expected to grow at a rate which will at least offset the decline in the industrial world. Thus, total NCW oil demand may be stagnant or, at most, increase minutely in the 1980s. The latest global energy forecast by the Exxon Corporation projects an annual oil demand growth rate of 0.3 percent for the NCW from 1979 to 1990. By comparison, in the eleven-year period ending in 1979 the growth rate was nearly 4 percent.

There are no resource or technical constraints in meeting a 1990 world demand level of this order of magnitude. It may not even require any increase in OPEC crude oil production from the 28.5 million B/D level maintained in the first half of 1980, when Iranian production was severely curtailed and most OPEC countries had spare capacity.[2]

Thus, it appears that in the next ten years, and probably beyond, no significant increase in the real price of oil will be required to keep demand from growing faster than economically available supply. Nevertheless, real prices may rise significantly during this period, since in the short and medium term the price elasticity of oil demand will remain below unity, giving oil exporters added real income from future price increases. In other words, attainment of a long-term equilibrium price provides no safeguard against increases above this price through successful market intervention in the form of price or production administration, such as OPEC has practiced in the past.

However, the spread between cost and sales price of any commodity cannot be increased indefinitely without eventually creating countervailing market forces. The demand developments referred to above are the first clear signs that these forces are gaining strength. Oil exporting countries with relatively small reserve potentials and a growing domestic demand for petroleum may be indifferent to these prospects, since such countries may cease to be major exporters before being affected by them.

2. OPEC natural gas liquids production (propane, butane, etc.) would have to increase significantly under this scenario. But this will occur in any case as a by-product of these countries' new natural gas production and utilization policy.

But countries which have the resource potential to remain substantial oil exporters into the next century may not be indifferent to the likely long-term effect of higher oil prices on their export demand. Saudi Arabia, Kuwait, Abu Dhabi, Venezuela (for its Orinoco oil belt) and Mexico are in that category, as, perhaps, is Iraq.

For these countries the short and medium term gains of further significant real price increases could be more than offset by long term declines, starting in the early or mid-1990s. The leaders and planners of these countries have frequently voiced concern about the post-oil era. So far, this has generally been defined as the period when there are no more exportable oil reserves. It has been said that the arrival of this period must be postponed by curtailing exports. This has inevitably contributed to the rise in world oil prices.

In view of the now clearly visible impact of the price increases of the last eight years on world oil consumption and on the development of substitute forms of energy, the leaders and planners of the major oil exporting countries may begin to consider the post-oil era as one in which their market for this commodity declines faster than their remaining reserves.

Displacing imported petroleum through conservation and substitution is primarily a function of economics and technology, the two, of course, being interrelated. OPEC has already provided more economic incentive than technology can cope with in the short run—hence, the current lag between oil price increases and the commercialization of new technologies. However, given enough time and a growing confidence that world oil prices will continue to rise in real terms, the industrial nations are likely to find technological answers to the problems of oil import reduction.

There is little evidence so far that these consequences of past and likely future oil price increases are being given serious consideration by OPEC members, although the consistently moderate oil pricing policy of Saudi Arabia, OPEC's super producer, probably reflects this consideration in part.

The reason for most OPEC members' apparent unconcern about these consequences may be their view that they control prices in both directions. Since the present price of OPEC oil is a high multiple of its actual production cost and will continue to remain so, OPEC and other oil exporters believe they can always protect their foreign markets simply by reducing their profit margins, if this should become necessary. This must be recognized as a valid argument. Certainly, the production cost of OPEC's exports is way below that of the new conventional and unconventional energy supplies developed to displace these exports.

However, the argument ignores the irreversible institutional changes brought about by OPEC's pricing policy. Substitution for and conservation of oil are some of these changes. Since the former is largely a function of changes in equipment design, it will continue for the foreseeable future, relatively unaffected by future price moderation. Another institutional change is likely to be government protection of high-cost domestic energy production from relatively low-cost foreign competition. There are plenty of precedents for this, such as the U.S. oil import policy from 1957 to 1973, the philosophic basis of which was the assumption that dependence on foreign oil presented a potential national security threat, independent of price, in view of the demonstrated insecurity of access to foreign oil.

Since the above factors are most applicable to the industrial countries, institutional forces can be expected to play an important part in the long-run irreversible reduction in oil import requirements in these countries.

To the extent to which exporters may want to offset this reduction they must find other outlets for their oil. Their own internal demand and that of the oil-importing LDC's provide such outlets on a rapidly growing scale. However, the prices obtainable in these markets may be lower than in the industrial countries. Most OPEC domestic oil markets are heavily subsidized (i.e. inland prices are substantially below export prices). For political and other reasons this rapidly growing market will continue to be subsidized.

The oil importing LDC's may only be able to import growing volumes of oil at rising prices if the exporters find some direct or indirect way to help finance these imports. On a small scale OPEC is already doing this through loans and grants. As these programs increase, OPEC will have to fund more of its exports in this manner. This future development poses a possible dilemma for OPEC: should export prices to the industrial countries be further raised to compensate for the growing share of OPEC oil going to subsidized markets, even if this accelerates the movement in these countries toward import substitution?

OPEC will not have to recognize this dilemma for the five–seven-year time span under consideration here. But the pricing decisions it makes during this period will in part determine how soon thereafter it will have to deal with the problem of a permanently shrinking premium market for its exports.

# Development Prospects in Arab Nations[1]

## By George T. Abed

### I. Introduction

THE SECOND ROUND of oil price increases in 1979 and early 1980 is likely
to shape the economic prospects of the Middle East in the 1980s much as
the 1973–74 oil-related events influenced the economic development of
the region in the 1970s. However, there are new factors in the emerging
global environment that are likely to complicate further the process of social and economic development in the region with important international implications.

In this paper I intend to outline the development prospects of the key
Arab countries of the Middle East[2] over the coming five years, highlighting the areas of potential achievement as well as those that could be the
cause of some concern.

### II. Recent Economic Developments

In discussing the economies of the six major oil exporting countries of the
Middle East, it is worth emphasizing the very special character of these
countries. Although in terms of per capita income these countries rank at
or near the top of a world scale, with a combined weighted average of
about $6,000 per capita, they still lack even the rudimentary elements of
a modern economy as reflected in a broad industrial base, a skilled labor force, and efficient service institutions. The other Arab countries of
the Middle East, although some are socially more developed, are much
poorer with a combined average per capita GNP of $500. This disparity
also reflects certain complementarities in social and economic conditions.

---

1. The views expressed in this paper are solely those of the author and in no way reflect
the positions or policies of the International Monetary Fund.

2. Countries covered in this paper are Egypt, Iraq, Jordan, Kuwait, Libya, Qatar, Saudi
Arabia, Syria, and the United Arab Emirates.

These, in turn, have created opportunities for intraregional flows of capital and labor which have expedited the development process considerably. Nearly 2.5 million Arabs from the poorer countries are residing and working in the Arab oil-exporting countries, sometimes constituting as much as 60 percent of the labor force and performing most essential tasks in industry and services. The reverse flow of capital, in the form of worker remittances, is running at about $4.5 billion annually and comprises a substantial portion of the nonoil countries' external receipts.

## The oil exporting countries[3]

The economic structure and recent developments in the oil exporting countries can be characterized as follows: the oil sector constitutes the larger share of real GDP, the ratio ranging from 50 percent for Libya to 78 percent for Qatar; the weighted average ratio for the six-country group was about 60 percent in 1979. Oil revenues constitute on average about 97 percent of total export revenues and about 90 percent of total budget receipts.

Rapid development and diversification of economic activity is directly linked to these economies' ability or willingness to import expatriate labor, even in such relatively more balanced economies as those of Iraq and Libya. Expatriate labor as a share of the total work force ranges from about 30 percent in Libya to 85 percent in Qatar and the United Arab Emirates.[4]

The structure of demand in these countries reflects the resource augmenting impact of oil exports, leading to unusually high savings and investment rates, despite rapid growth of consumption. Although consumption growth averaged about 30 percent over the 1975–79 period, the proportion of GDP devoted to investment has remained substantial, averaging about 27 percent in recent years.

All six countries launched rather ambitious development plans from the mid-1970s onwards. Some of these plans represented quantum leaps over previous plans—between three and ten times. All development plans were built on the twin themes of rapid economic growth and diversification, although the latter often meant investment in downstream oil and gas operations. In all cases, growth of nonoil GDP was set much higher than that of the oil sector (roughly twice or more), leading to projected declines in the share of the oil sector in real GDP. For the five

3. The six countries other than Egypt, Jordan, and Syria noted in footnote 2.
4. No data are available on the composition of the labor force in Iraq, but expatriates are thought not to exceed 12–15 percent of the labor force.

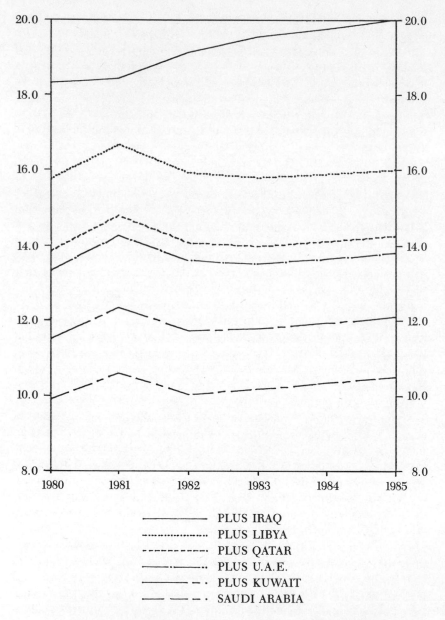

PLUS IRAQ
PLUS LIBYA
PLUS QATAR
PLUS U.A.E.
PLUS KUWAIT
SAUDI ARABIA

**Fig. 2. Arab Oil-Exporting Countries—Oil Production**
*(in millions of barrels per day)*

years 1975–80, total planned expenditures for the six countries were set at about $40 billion annually, or about $150,000 for each job created, with expenditures in the latter years of the plans being higher still. Of the total planned outlays, approximately 40 percent was devoted to the commodity producing sectors, 35 percent to infrastructure, and 25 percent to services.

All the countries in question succeeded initially in rapidly increasing their domestic expenditure levels and generally achieving high rates of growth. However, ambitious expenditure plans soon ran up against domestic supply constraints, especially manpower, infrastructure, and managerial resources, and real growth rates slowed down toward the end of the period. In addition, because of worldwide slackening of demand for oil, oil prices and export receipts stagnated in 1977 and 1978, leading most governments to adopt more restrictive demand management policies and to limit the inflows of immigrant workers. Measures to expand resource supplies were also instituted and, together with deflationary demand policies, helped contain inflationary pressures. Saudi Arabia was particularly successful in this respect where the rate of growth of the nonoil GDP deflator was reduced from 41 percent in 1975 to about 7 percent in 1979.

Oil exports of the six oil exporting countries rose most dramatically from $18.3 billion in 1973 to $129.1 billion in 1979 and were estimated at about $200 billion in 1980. Correspondingly, imports increased from $6.8 billion in 1973 to $52.2 billion in 1979 and were estimated at $75 billion for 1980. About 60 percent of all recorded merchandise imports consisted of foods and raw materials and the remaining 40 percent of capital goods. The current account surplus of the six countries rose from $6.7 billion in 1973 to $43.3 billion in 1974, but declined to $19.7 billion by 1978. It then rose to $57.6 billion in 1979 and to about $100 billion in 1980. Gross monetary reserves increased from $7.7 billion in 1973 to an estimated $42.0 billion at the end of June 1980, equivalent to about seven months of imports at the projected 1980 level. Official net foreign assets also rose dramatically and are estimated, unofficially, to have amounted to about $285 billion by the end of 1980.[5]

During the period 1974–79, the six Arab oil-exporting countries bilaterally provided nearly $30 billion in concessional financial assistance to developing countries, the annual flow amounting to between 2.5 and 5.0 percent of their combined GNP.[6] This is in addition to these countries' financial participation in lending facilities in regional and international or-

5. See for example Susan Bluff, "OPEC's $350 Billion Balance Sheet," *Euromoney* (Sept. 1980), 116 and *Business Week* (7 Oct. 1980) 70–84.

6. OPEC data: OECD data tend to show lower levels of aid because of a more restrictive

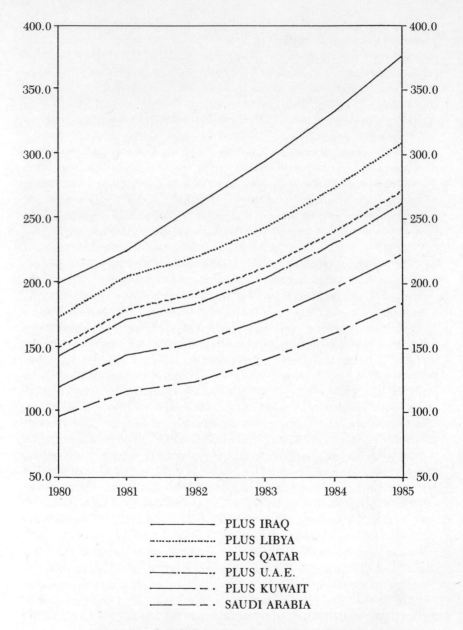

Fig. 3. Arab Oil-Exporting Countries—Exports
*(in billions of U.S. dollars)*

ganizations (e.g., Arab Fund, OPEC Special Fund, the International Monetary Fund, and World Bank).

## The nonoil countries

The economic profile of the three nonoil countries (Egypt, Jordan, and Syria) is more akin to that of other middle-income, developing countries (World Bank classification). The main features of their economic structures and recent developments can be summarized in the following: the resource base and the structure of production are somewhat more balanced, with substantial shares of GDP attributable to agriculture, industry, and services. On average, about 20 percent of GDP originates in agriculture (Jordan having the lowest share at 11 percent), 30 percent in industry, and 50 percent in services. This pattern matches a level of development somewhat below the average for the middle-income countries. The labor force structure, on the other hand, is about average for this group of countries with about 40 percent of the employment in agriculture, 30 percent in industry, and 30 percent in the service sectors.

Two of the three countries (Egypt and Syria) have based their economic development on the assignment of a strong, and in some sectors dominant, role to the public sector, especially in industry, trade, and in the control of investment funds. However, since 1974, Egypt has departed markedly from this pattern but the role of the public sector, although no longer dominant, remains quite important. Jordan has followed a pragmatic, mixed-sector policy, permitting the private sector to play an important role; in the process it has achieved relatively high growth rates despite the paucity of natural resources (other than human capital). By comparison, Egypt and Syria both have large, and generally inefficient, public economic sectors which have not made a measurable contribution to the economic development of these two economies. Also, both of these countries have committed themselves to ambitious (given their limited resources) social welfare policies which have increasingly become a strain on available resources. In Egypt direct subsidies amount to about 12 percent of GDP, probably the highest ratio in the world. Indirect subsidies and cost-price distortions consume inordinate proportions of total resources in the two countries.

All three countries have adopted sizeable five-year development plans with total annual expenditures planned at $9.2 billion or about $25,000

---

definition of consessionality. See for example *Middle East Economic Survey* (4 Feb. 1980), Table 16, p. 000 for OECD data.

for each new job created. Of the total resources about 35 percent on average was intended for the commodity sectors, 45 percent for infrastructure, and 20 percent for services. In all three countries, national savings are insufficient to finance the development effort and all three rely heavily on remittances and aid inflows; in the case of Egypt, service export receipts from the Suez Canal and from tourism also play an important role. It is worth noting that both Syria and Egypt are net exporters of crude oil and, in light of recent sharp increases in oil prices, oil revenues have become important sources of export receipts and budgetary income.

In part because of the easing of external financial constraints and the spillover from the oil boom that has swept the Middle East region, real rates of growth of GDP in all three countries have been relatively high— 7–9 percent annually, about 2–3 times the average comparable rate for the middle-income, developing countries and on par with the oil exporting countries themselves. As in the case of the oil exporting countries, growth rates tended to subside in 1977 and 1978.

Concerning the external sector, all three countries have chronic (and entirely understandable) current account deficits. However, these deficits have been nearly offset by capital inflows (mainly in the form of official transfers and, in the case of Egypt and Jordan, direct investment) so that, in the past three years, these three countries have moved their balance of payments positions to small surpluses or at least overall balance—a remarkable result for countries whose merchandise exports, on average, cover only about 40 percent of their imports.

The external reserve positions of these three countries have also improved appreciably despite considerable increases in imports and in development expenditures. Such reserves stood at $2.9 billion at the end of June 1980, equivalent to about 2.5 months of imports at the projected 1980 level. External public debt and debt service payments are relatively high, although not yet worrisome, for Egypt; while for Jordan and Syria they are at or below the average of the middle-income, developing countries.

## III. Development Prospects in 1980s[7]

Development prospects in the Arab oil-exporting countries through 1985 are likely to follow a time pattern broadly similar to the one that prevailed

7. All projections in this section, made in November 1980, represent the author's own views at the time and in no way reflect the official outlook of the IMF.

immediately after the 1973–74 oil price increases. Growth is therefore likely to be vigorous through 1982 or 1983 but is expected to subside somewhat beyond that, although not as precipitously as it did in 1977–78.

For purposes of the projections to 1985 used here, I have assumed that oil production from these six countries will rise only marginally by 1985— on the order of an additional 1.5 mbd over the 18.6 mbd average rate of production recorded in January–July 1980. Underlying this forecast is the assumption that world-oil demand in general will rise by 1985 only marginally above its 1980 levels and that most of the new production will come from countries other than the six countries discussed here. Furthermore, production from Iraq is assumed to recover only slowly in early 1981 and to reach prewar capacity no earlier than mid-1981.

As to oil prices, a number of plausible scenarios are possible and, in fact, judging from recent experience, almost anything is possible. However, I have used the assumption that oil prices will rise annually through 1985 by 3 percent in real terms or by 12 percent in nominal terms, so that the nominal price of oil will be about $54 per barrel by the end of the period. It can be argued that this assumption may be somewhat conservative in view of more recent events both on the assumed real oil price increase and on the projected underlying inflation rate (9 per cent); oil prices and oil revenues could therefore rise rather more rapidly, especially after the current slump in demand is over, perhaps in the second half of 1981.

For the nonoil countries the annual real growth rates of GNP to 1985 are assumed at 7.5 percent for Egypt, 6.5 percent for Jordan, and 5.0 percent for Syria. All these rates are lower than those achieved by these three countries in recent years (8.5 percent, 7.6 percent, and 7.8 percent, respectively, in the period 1974–79), but I am projecting some slowdown toward the end of the period, from the somewhat higher rates prevailing now. As for the balance of payments estimates for these countries, I have assumed "normal" export growth with the same oil price assumptions in the case of Egypt and Syria as I used for the oil exporting countries. Import elasticities are derived from recent experience and the import profile is assumed to have a shape similar to that of the rate of growth, as imports are assumed to be determined by GDP.

The salient features of the projections based on these and other subsidiary assumptions are summarized below.

Growth rates in the six oil-exporting countries will be generally lower than in the boom years of the 1970s. Two main factors account for this. In the first place, because of the projected slack in world-oil demand, rates of growth in the oil sectors will be much lower—about 2.0 percent *vs* 6.5

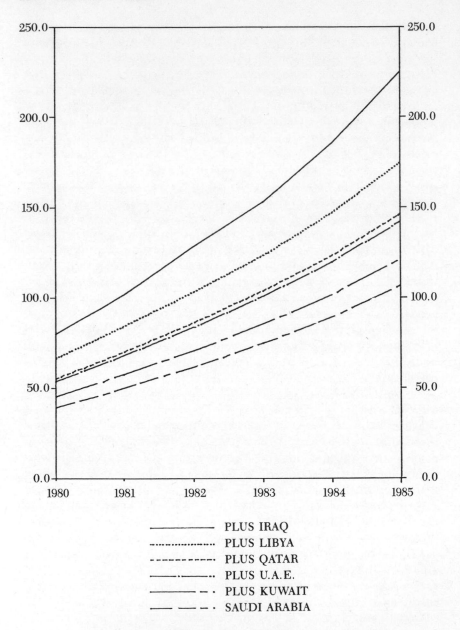

Fig. 4. Arab Oil-Exporting Countries—Imports
*(in billions of U.S. dollars)*

percent in the 1975–79 period. Secondly, growth rates are projected to subside in the later years, say in 1983 and 1984, because of the likelihood that domestic supply constraints, especially manpower, could begin to be a limiting factor. In the oil countries, emphasis will be increasingly shifted from infrastructure toward the commodity producing sectors, especially energy-based industries.

In all six countries, the oil sector is likely to grow at slower rates than the non-oil sectors so that diversification in the structure of GDP will continue.

As for the development of the external sector, exports are expected to grow in line with the exports of oil (marginal volume increases together with 12 percent growth in nominal oil prices) while imports are projected to rise by 18–30 percent annually, with higher rates recorded in the earlier years than in the later ones. On this basis, total exports of the six countries will be about $376 billion in 1985 compared to $198 billion in 1980, and imports nearly three times as large—$225 billion compared to $78 billion in 1980. One interesting feature of the oil-exporting countries' balance of payments is the steady increase in service receipts, mainly from investment income, which is projected to rise from about $18 billion in 1980 to nearly $48 billion in 1985.

The six oil exporting countries are expected to continue to record current account surpluses throughout the 1980–85 period, with the surplus in 1985 projected at $82.5 billion.[8]

Net official foreign assets of the six countries are likely to rise from about $210 billion in 1979 to about $565 billion in 1985.

The three nonoil countries' external positions will weaken considerably over the coming five years because of continued deterioration of their trade accounts. Exports are projected to rise at 12–18 percent annually while imports are expected to increase at 15–24 percent per year, leading to a widening of the trade deficit from an estimated $7.25 billion in 1980 to about $20.0 billion in 1985. All three are large recipients of remittances and of official aid transfers so that service receipts and capital inflows will offset, to some extent, the large trade deficits. Nonetheless, their combined overall balance of payments position is expected to deteriorate from its present equilibrium status.

The spillover effects of developments in the oil countries into the nonoil countries of the region will continue, and it is unlikely that any of the

8. Other OPEC members are expected to be in deficit so that the OPEC surplus as a whole will be much smaller.

three countries in the latter group will experience severe foreign exchange constraints for the next three–four years. However, in the case of Egypt, in the absence of new oil discoveries, external constraints could begin to take effect before 1985 if current trends continue, so that its high rates of investment and consumption growth could be threatened, possibly by 1984, and not later than 1985. In the absence of continued increases in external aid receipts, Syria could also run up against foreign exchange constraints at about that time.

## IV. The Road Ahead

It is clear from the foregoing that, on purely economic grounds, none of the nine countries examined is likely to face serious difficulties in the period ahead. Indeed, on the face of it, the economic prospects even for the nonoil countries look promising—real per capita income will continue to rise and development plans are not likely to be threatened by severe shortages of funds. In the case of the oil exporting countries, growth rates will remain high, diversification will proceed further and their external financial assets will continue to rise.

It is worth noting, however, that at least some of the countries concerned will continue to exhibit weaknesses in their economic structures which could make them vulnerable. In the nonoil countries these weaknesses are reflected in heavy dependence on external aid to finance rising levels of imports, low productivity in the traditional sectors of agriculture and industry, cost-price distortions leading to misallocation of resources, low domestic saving ratios and generally inflexible fiscal structures. High levels of domestic expenditures, financed in great part from external receipts, have led to rising inflationary pressures and to further aggravation of cost-price distortions, especially in the two countries where rigid pricing policies have hampered the development of effective supply response mechanisms. In the oil-exporting countries, a revival of a high-spending, high-growth development strategy could intensify inflationary pressures and cause economic and possibly social disruptions. Fortunately, most of these countries appear to have learned the lessons of the boom years of the mid-1970s and are proceeding more cautiously this time around.

However, if one were to look at the prospects for the *oil exporting countries* in a broader social and political context, a number of problems tend to emerge, some of which could have far-reaching consequences. I will briefly touch upon some of the more important ones.

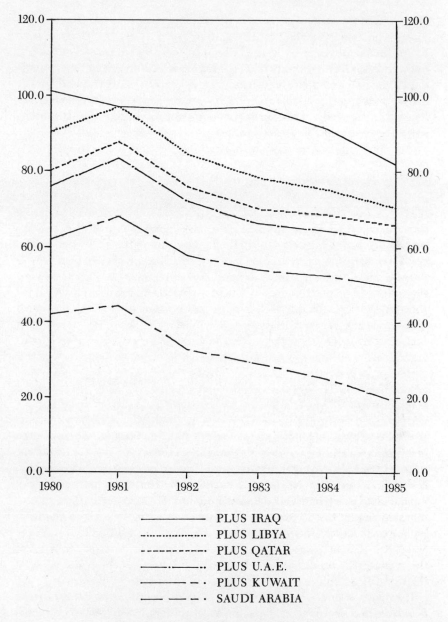

**Fig. 5. Arab Oil-Exporting Countries—
current account balances**

### The widening divergence between economic modernization and social and political underdevelopment

This phenomenon manifests itself in the establishment of the most modern, economic and financial institutions in a milieu so traditional that it tends to highlight certain social inconsistencies and, possibly, contradictions. Because of the intensity of the modernization drive and the potential strength of opposing social forces, extreme solutions could emerge. The social tension that could develop must be handled most judiciously.

### The impact of high levels of expenditures on internal cohesion

Two aspects are worth mentioning: the impact on income distribution: although data are not available, there are indications that rapid accumulation of wealth in certain countries could have an adverse impact on the distribution of income, not only within these countries but also among the countries of the region as well; and the increasing "Westernization" of consumption (as well as of investment) patterns and lifestyles carries with it the potential for increased alienation of the traditional sections of the population.

### The political clash between the concentration of economic control in the central governments and the liberating impact of modernization

In the oil exporting countries, the public sector controls the source of all economic power—oil. As development and education begin to take root, demands for democratization, in the full sense of the term, are likely to become stronger. Unless indigenous political institutions are quickly developed and are permitted to function effectively, the challenge to the increasing powers of the central authority could ultimately cause a rupture in the social fabric of these societies.

### The increasingly dualistic character of the oil-based societies

The most evident manifestation of dualism is in the distinction between nationals and expatriates. Although the latter may have been born in and spent much of their useful lives in the service of their host countries,

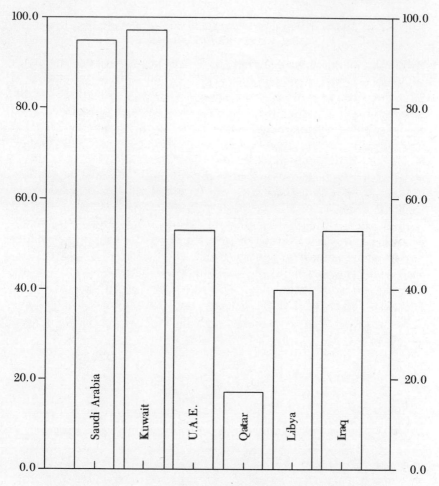

**Fig. 6. Increases in official net foreign assets, 1980–1985**
*(in billions of U.S. dollars)*

the fact is that, at least in some of the oil-exporting countries, expatriates cannot own property, do not exercise any political rights, and receive a truncated version of the social benefits available to the native population. Although from the standpoint of the host countries such policies and attitudes may be understandable, nonetheless, as a result, most expatriates tend to hold to national or ethnic loyalties that are exogenous to the host countries.

Rising dissatisfaction with current oil depletion
and asset accumulation rates

Within the oil exporting countries, those who argue for more restrained oil-production rates, commensurate with the national requirements of the oil-exporting countries themselves, are gaining strength and could conceivably prevail within the political power structure (as has already occurred in some oil-exporting countries). Although, because of conservation and improved supplies of energy from other sources, Middle East oil no longer plays the life-or-death role it once played in the early 1970s, nonetheless, the regional and international implications of an extreme version of a purely nationalistic attitude in the oil exporting countries could be serious.

To some extent, many of these observations are not unique to the oil-exporting countries; in various degrees they could well apply to a number of developing countries, some of which have managed to industrialize successfully. The possibility of success in the Arab oil-exporting countries is not foreclosed here, but the pitfalls in the road ahead should give policymakers and students of the region grounds for some serious reflection.

# The Hard Realities of Arab Development

### By Odeh F. Aburdene

Mr. Abed has done a superb job in highlighting the development prospects and their potential positive as well as negative impact over the coming five years. Mr. Abed is correct in stating that most of the Gulf oil exporting countries (excluding Iraq) still lack the rudimentary elements of a modern economy, as reflected in a broad industrial and agricultural base, a skilled and motivated labor force, and efficient service institutions. The economic structure of these countries will not change dramatically over the coming five years and will continue to be characterized as follows: 1) Foreign labor will constitute over 70 percent of the labor force. 2) Agriculture is practically nonexistent (Iraq being an exception). 3) The bulk of the industry that will come on stream will be oil related. 4) Oil and oil-related products will constitute the larger share of GDP and nearly 97 percent of total exports.

The inflow of large oil revenues to these states in the future will not transform them into industrially advanced countries. Their economic power is not only small, but the foundation of that power is too narrow and vulnerable, being based on the export of a single depletable resource. Moreover, this economic power does not translate into military power of international significance. Without oil, the Gulf region is the poorest region of the globe because it lacks industry, agriculture, water and manpower.

As Mr. Abed has indicated, the Middle East has a huge diversity of capabilities among states: some have large financial resources but a small labor force, others have arable land but insufficient capital for agricultural development, and others have trained workers but too few jobs. Regional development seems to make good economic sense; however, political, communal, religious and economic disparities make regional development impossible.

Mr. Abed touched on two issues that will have a major impact on these countries as well as on the outside world. These issues are the consequence of internal growth and the buildup of substantial foreign reserves abroad. The most decisive issues in the coming years will be determined by whether the Gulf countries will translate oil surpluses into development to achieve greater sectoral balance and diversification and to maximize human resources. The availability of capital has allowed these countries to substitute imports for domestic labor, food, and technology, and the next five years will not bring a major change. Development cannot be imported as a prefabricated package. Development is not just glistening new asphalt highways, shiny new buildings and air-conditioned business centers; nor is it just sending people to college because it is prestigious to do so.

What is taking place in the Gulf today cannot be called effective development. It is growth without development. Effective development involves more than having money; it involves a complex change of attitudes towards living in towns, working in industry, accepting responsibilities, making decisions, and changing major enterprises. Moreover, development begins with people. The Gulf countries have very few people. These countries are not keen on waves of immigrants coming to help with their nation-building, as happened in the U.S. in the 19th century. The oil nations are nervous about the possibility that foreigners' skills and ambition will show up or overwhelm the native populations. You cannot have development when foreigners, on average, make up 70 percent of the work force and are daily reminded that they will never be assimilated. Without assimilating foreigners, you do not earn their loyalty nor increase their productivity. As one Saudi official put it: "We welcome the foreigners, we need them, their technology and their labor. We don't, however, need their social and cultural input into our society. They are a threat to our morals and traditions." Finally, you cannot have economic modernization when most of the native population is not involved, in an occupational sense, in the development process.

Since none of these governments have either firmly implanted institutions or widely accepted political symbols, high growth, rather than development, also carries unforeseen social and political risks in the years ahead. As cosmetic economic growth proceeds, new socio-economic tensions within these countries will aggravate long-standing religious and communal antagonisms. The processes of education, urbanization, and alienation of the foreign labor force, mixing with corruption, could produce an explosive environment. All these factors combined with the buildup of strong armies will stimulate instability and enhance the possibility of the military staging a coup d'etat. The Arab-Israeli conflict, as well as the Iraqi-Iranian war, are likely to reinforce the forces of divisiveness in the Gulf. Thus, the coming years would appear to be ones of domestic tension and instability.

The economic relationship between the oil-exporting countries and the oil-importing countries of the West will become more pivotal in the next five years. The oil producers and the advanced countries are caught up in an economic relationship from which neither can escape. The West needs oil and cooperation in managing the international monetary system. The oil nations seek goods and services, military technology, and investment opportunities from the industrially more advanced West to accommodate the $600 billion that they will accumulate by 1985. Before we talk about the future, let us look at what has happened since 1973.

At the end of 1973, when oil prices were raised by OPEC, there was considerable speculation in the Western press about how the oil-producing countries would use the receipts they obtained from the sale of oil at higher prices. At the time, there were dire forecasts of OPEC, particularly its Arab members, slowly but systematically buying the major companies of the world. The list of possible investments included Krupp, IBM, General Motors, DuPont, Exxon, *the New York Times*, CBS and others. Moreover, renowned experts asserted that the accumulation of external assets by the oil nations would be critical for the existing monetary system. They stated that "there will be monetary disorders when large holders speculate against a particular currency. Unlike the oil market, where the producing countries must act in concert or accomplish nothing, even a single nation with big enough foreign balances can do substantial damage to the world monetary system, or try to bring down a government it dislikes." While these anxieties were being expressed, Mr. Abdul Latif al-Hamad, general director of the Kuwait fund for Arab economic development, cautioned: "One issue has been increasingly on our minds. . . . This concerns continuous erosion in the value of Arab investment portfolio, an erosion that has unfortunately reached alarming proportions if account is taken of the successive devaluations of the world's once most prestigious reserve currencies, as well as of the world-wide spiral of inflation and the rapid decline in the purchasing power of money."

Time dissipated many of the worries and anxieties which troubled and concerned investors, policy makers, journalists, and academicians and vindicated Mr. al-Hamad. In fact, so far, OPEC has been exceedingly cautious and conservative. The OPEC nations did not engage in financial maneuvers to upset the economies of those countries where their oil is sold and where their funds are invested, nor did they buy the major companies of the world.

The OPEC countries want to turn their financial assets into something that has a solid underlying capital value and not just a big portfolio that is producing a return. Thus, the placement of deposits in banks and the holding of U.S. government obligations, as well as corporate bonds and stocks, must be seen, at most, as transitory investments during the lag between receipt of oil revenues and their expenditure for development and industrialization. OPEC countries have treated their surpluses as a "pension fund," and have therefore had to evolve a serious investment policy, designed, as Mr. Khaled Abu Said, chief investment advisor to the government of Kuwait, put it, "to maintain the real value of those assets in order to guarantee a reasonable inheritance to the coming generations who will see the continuing depletion of our oil resources." The dilemma faced by the oil producing countries, which could become acute if they ever decide to shift to a strategy of long-range, solid investments to provide an income for future generations, was aptly expressed by Abdullah Saudi, the chief executive of the Arab Banking Corporation (owned by Kuwait, the U.A.E. and Libya): "If I invest in short-term deposits, I am criticized for keeping my investments in hot money, and if I go long, I am accused of trying to take over the world."

Many of us here in the West tend to regard our annual oil revenues as income, in the same category as the income from the sale of corn or Pepsi Cola. However, oil, unlike corn or Pepsi Cola, is a depletable finite commodity which will someday disappear. Thus it is an asset or capital. The surplus funds that remain after payments for imports of goods and services and foreign grants are assets. We cannot go on asking the oil producing countries to export more oil and, at the same time, express dire concern about the buildup of foreign exchange reserves. It is clear that there would be no surplus revenues at all if the oil production of the Gulf states were a function of economic need. To do this, of course, would not only spell ruin for the Western economies and, consequently, the Gulf states themselves, but might even lead to the seizure of their foreign assets as well as their oil fields. The big question that we must ask in the coming years is how the Western economies can accommodate the sizable savings of the oil exporting countries. If these countries are to go on producing around the current level over the next five years, we must devise a way that will make the oil surpluses both "financially secure and politically acceptable to the West." Financial security means protection against inflation, currency fluctuations, and seizure.

# International Migration, Manpower and Economic Growth in the Arab Region

## By J. S. Birks, C. A. Sinclair and J. A. Socknat[1]

### A. Labor Migration in the Region[2]

### I. Introduction

IN THE OIL EXPORTING COUNTRIES of the Middle East and North Africa,[3] the sharp increase in revenues following the price rises of 1973 substantially eased or, in some cases, practically eliminated the financial constraints to economic growth. Yet, this novel development brought with it difficult issues for policy makers. Apart from socio-political choices like the appropriate role of the public and private sectors, standards of income distribution, industrial diversification and rate of oil depletion, they had

1. The views and interpretations in this document are those of the authors and should not be attributed to the World Bank.
2. This paper is abstracted from a report which presents the interim findings of a World Bank funded research project on Labor Migration and Manpower in the Middle East and North Africa. It covers an assessment of the region's labor migration status in 1975 and one round of projections to 1985 of manpower requirements and supply for eight major oil-endowed, labor-importing countries in the region. The research project was initiated jointly by the Development Economics Department (DED) and the Europe, Middle East, and North Africa (EMENA) Region. It is being executed by the Technical Assistance and Special Studies Division of the EMENA projects Department (EMP), under the direction of Mr. Ismail Serageldin, Chief, TASS Division. A substantive contribution to this early phase of the project was made by Zafer Ecevit. Other individuals contributing to the study included: Bob Li, Mirta Halperin, Mary Markowitz, Qaiser Khan. Results of the study as contained in this interim report are subject to revision/modification as work on the study proceeds. The figures provided in this report should be read as provisional orders of magnitude. It should be noted that the views and interpretations in this paper are those of the authors and should not be attributed to the World Bank, to its affiliated organizations, or to any individual acting on their behalf.
3. The eight major Arab oil-exporting countries covered by this report are: Algeria, Bahrain, Kuwait, Libya, Oman, Qatar, Saudi Arabia, and the United Arab Emirates.

the difficult task of mobilizing other factors of production. Absorption of the new scale of government revenues and, therefore, economic growth, was impeded by a general lack of infrastructure, but more importantly by an acute shortage of manpower at all skill levels.

Since 1973 the oil-exporting countries of the region have been able to invest heavily, initially in physical and social infrastructure, and later in industry and services, partly by virtue of large scale expatriate labor imports. However, increasing concern has been manifested over the size and growth of the expatriate populations and their socio-political implications.

The non oil endowed countries of the Middle East and South Asia met the bulk of this demand for labor, often competing with one another and, in certain cases, at the expense of draining their pool of productively employed skilled manpower. Consequently, the Middle East labor market has emerged as one of the major policy issues for most countries in the region; its importance virtually parallels the commodity and manufacturer's markets. In fact, labor flows have reached such a scale that it has now become very difficult to assess the prospects for economic growth in many of these labor importing and labor exporting countries without a good understanding of the Middle East labor market.

## II. The Magnitude, Source, and Destination of Migrant Labor Flows, 1975

In 1975, there were almost 2 million migrant workers in the oil-exporting countries in the Middle East and North Africa. In several oil exporting countries in the region, migrant workers outnumbered the indigenous labor force by large margins. Thus, although in 1975 the expatriate share of total employment in the region was 11 percent, in certain of the oil-exporting countries the expatriate share of employment was much higher.

The unusually high dependence upon migrant labor in the oil-exporting states can be traced to their small indigenous populations, the limited educational attainment of these populations, and their low labor force participation rates. These low participation rates stem from the youthful population structures in the oil-exporting countries (meaning that a large proportion of the total population is too young to enter the labor force) compounded by the recent expansion in higher education, which is temporarily holding back many potential entrants to the labor market. Also significant are the low overall female labor-participation rates. Only those oil-exporting countries with relatively larger populations or more mature education systems managed to hold down the expatriate component of

## Table 7

Origin of Migrant Labor in the Middle East and North Africa, 1975
(*in thousands*)

| Source | Total | % |
|---|---|---|
| Egypt | 298.1 | 16.1 |
| Jordan | 134.6 | 7.3 |
| Morocco | 2.2 | 0.1 |
| Oman | 18.6 | 1.0 |
| Somalia | 5.2 | 0.3 |
| Sudan | 19.9 | 1.1 |
| Syria | 51.3 | 2.8 |
| Tunisia | 29.2 | 1.6 |
| Yemen Arab Republic | 469.4 | 25.3 |
| P.D.R. Yemen | 69.4 | 3.7 |
| Europe & North America | 133.7 | 7.2 |
| India | 160.5 | 8.7 |
| Pakistan | 171.0 | 9.2 |
| Others | 289.2 | 15.6 |
| Total Expatriates | 1,852.3 | 100.0 |

*Source*: A wide variety of primary and secondary data sources have been used in the compilation of these tables, which comprise the base year data for projections through 1985.

their employment in 1975 to within the range experienced in Europe.

In 1975, 59 percent of the total migrant workforce in the oil-exporting countries of the region was provided by ten Arab countries, namely: Yemen Arab Republic, 25.2 percent; Egypt, 16.1 percent; Jordan, 7.3 percent; P.D.R. of Yemen, 3.7 percent; Morocco, 0.1 percent; Oman, 1.0 percent; Somalia, 0.3 percent; Sudan, 1.1 percent; Syria, 2.8 percent; Tunisia, 1.6 percent. The Indian subcontinent was the second largest source of labor; India and Pakistan together supplied about 18 percent of the total, with heavy concentrations working in the Arabian peninsula. The share of Europe (including Eastern Europe) and North America was close to 7 percent. The remaining 16 percent of expatriate workers came from Afghanistan, Bangladesh, Turkey, Korea, the Philippines, and other countries in Africa and East Asia (Table 7).

International labor flows to and within the Arab world have increased substantially since 1975. Although Arab labor experts did increase between 1975 and 1979, particularly from Egypt and Jordan, it was increased imports of workers from South and South East Asia to the Arab world which provided an increasing proportion of new supplies. Bangladesh entered the market in late 1975 and had sent close to 75,000 workers to the region by the end of 1978. The most dramatic change in this pattern since 1975 has been the increasing role of South East Asian countries, namely Korea, Philippines, and, to a lesser extent, Indonesia, Thailand and Sri Lanka. These countries entered the Middle East labor market through national contracting firms which brought the labor components of the project, established "work camps" for the duration of the project, and provided most of the basic services (housing, utilities, health services, etc.) themselves. The "work camp" approach to labor recruitment lowered recruitment costs and alleviated pressures on housing and other basic services.

### III. Sectoral and Occupational Characteristics of Migrant Workers in 1975

In 1975, out of the 1.6 million migrant workers in the major labor-importing countries of Algeria, Bahrain, Kuwait, Libya, Oman, Qatar, Saudi Arabia and the UAE,[4] the largest proportion (35 percent), were employed in the construction sector, followed by services (23 percent), trade and finance (15 percent), and agriculture (8 percent). Relatively smaller proportions were employed in utilities (2 percent), mining and quarrying, which is predominantly hydrocarbons (2 percent), manufacturing (6 percent), and transportation and communications (7 percent). Details are shown in Table 8.

Among the factors accounting for the sectoral composition of the expatriate workforce in the labor-importing countries are the country-specific degrees of quantitative and qualitative deficiencies in the indigenous labor force as well as the deployment patterns of available nationals. As can be seen in Table 8, in the eight major Arab labor-importing states, approximately 27 percent of all jobs were held by expatriates in 1975. The share of employment accounted for by nonnationals was greatest in the construction sector (62 percent), followed by utilities (42 percent), trade and finance (41 percent), and transportation and communications (38 percent).

Comparison of deployment patterns of nationals among sectors is most easily made by using representation indexes. Table 9 shows that a reasonably consistent pattern of deployment of national labor force participants among the sectors prevailed in 1975 in the eight major Arab labor-import-

---

4. These 1.6 million represent the major proportion of the total 1.85 million workers recorded for the whole region in Table 7.

## Table 8

Distribution and Share of Expatriate Employment by Sector
in the Major Labor-Importing Countries, 1975

| Economic Sectors | Expatriates' Distribution of Employment | | Expatriates' Share of Employment |
|---|---|---|---|
| | No. | % | % |
| Agriculture | 148,400 | 8.9 | 6.5 |
| Mining & Quarrying | 32,500 | 2.0 | 28.2 |
| Manufacturing | 104,400 | 6.3 | 26.2 |
| Utilities | 26,200 | 1.6 | 41.8 |
| Construction | 588,200 | 35.3 | 62.2 |
| Trade & Finance | 250,900 | 15.1 | 40.9 |
| Transportation & Communications | 118,900 | 7.2 | 38.1 |
| Services | 391,700 | 23.6 | 26.8 |
| TOTAL | 1,661,200 | 100.0 | 26.7 |

*Source*: Base year data of the projections.
Notes: The total of expatriates in this table varies from that in Table 7 because this table is restricted to the eight major oil exporting states under study.

ing countries. Agriculture had the highest representation of nationals, ranging from one to just over three times their respective nationals' share of total employment. Services, primarily because of the public administration component of this sector, also showed a high incidence of nationals, ranging from one to something under two times the nationals' shares of total employment. Sectors in which nationals were most underrepresented were construction and manufacturing. In some labor-importing states construction sector jobs are nearly completely filled by expatriates.

In terms of the occupational composition of expatriate workers in 1975, the majority were engaged in unskilled (26 percent) or semiskilled (28 percent) occupations. Another 26 percent were employed in skilled office and manual occupations (Table 10).

Although nonnational workers in professional and (science based) technician occupations constituted a quantitatively minor share of total nonnational labor stocks, they account for very substantial shares of employment in these occupations: professional-technical (62 percent), other professional (54 percent), and technician (40 percent) for the labor-importing countries in 1975 (Table 10).

## Table 9

### Representation Indexes of Nationals' Employment in the Eight Major Arab Labor-Importing Countries by Sector, 1975

| Sector | Range | (Median Point) | Unweighted Average |
|---|---|---|---|
| Agriculture | 1.00–3.08 | (1.54) | 1.69 |
| Services | 1.00–1.80 | (1.19) | 1.29 |
| Transportation & Communications | 0.62–1.63 | (1.13) | 1.13 |
| Utilities | 0.41–1.64 | (1.12) | 1.11 |
| Mining & Quarrying | 0.35–1.26 | (1.00) | 1.02 |
| Trade & Finance | 0.43–1.00 | (0.63) | 0.71 |
| Manufacturing | 0.06–1.00 | (0.56) | 0.57 |
| Construction | 0.16–1.00 | (0.35) | 0.45 |

Notes: For each country, nationals' share of total labor force = 1.00

## Table 10

### Occupational Distribution of Expatriate Workers and Their Share of Total Employment, by Occupation, in the Eight Major Labor-Importing Countries, 1975

| Occupational Groupings | Occupational Distribution of Expatriate Workers | | Expatriates' Share of Total Employment |
|---|---|---|---|
| | No. | % | % |
| A–1 Professional-Technical Occupations | 67,900 | 4.1 | 61.6 |
| A–2 Other Professional Occupations | 134,000 | 8.1 | 53.6 |
| B–1 Technical Occupations | 76,800 | 4.6 | 40.4 |
| B–2 Other Subprofessional Occupations | 55,400 | 3.3 | 22.2 |
| C–1 Skilled Office & Manual Occupations | 425,800 | 25.6 | 46.1 |
| C–2 Semiskilled & Manual Occupations | 471,600 | 28.4 | 26.9 |
| D   Unskilled Occupations | 429,700 | 25.9 | 15.7 |
| Total | 1,661,200 | 100.0 | 26.7 |

*Source*: Base year data of the projections.

## Table 11

Representation Indexes of Nationals' Employment in
Labor-Importing Countries, by Occupation, 1975

| Occupation | Range (Median Point) | Unweighted Average |
|---|---|---|
| B–2: Other Subprofessional Occupations | 0.63–1.67 (1.13) | 1.16 |
| C–2: Semiskilled Office & Manual Occupations | 0.57–1.51 (1.05) | 1.11 |
| C–1: Skilled Office & Manual Occupations | 0.39–1.93 (1.00) | 1.09 |
| D    : Unskilled Occupations | 0.70–1.41 (0.90) | 0.94 |
| A–2: Other Professional Occupations | 0.69–1.15 (0.93) | 0.93 |
| B–1: Technician Occupations | 0.26–0.97 (0.62) | 0.65 |
| A–1: Professsional-Technical Occupations | 0.27–0.96 (0.37) | 0.47 |

Notes: For each country, nationals' share of total labor force = 1.00

The pattern of relative severity of shortages of nationals available for the various occupational categories in 1975 can be seen in Table 11. It shows that among the eight major Arab labor-importing countries the lowest incidences of nationals (and consequently the most severe requirements for and dependence upon expatriates) were, as might be expected, in the professional occupations, (science based) technician occupations, and other professional occupations. Given the rigidity of education/training prerequisites for employment in these occupations and the nascent state of postsecondary and university education systems in the labor-importing countries, this pattern is likely to remain significant for some years, despite the major educational effort being mounted in these states.

Table 12 shows the share of employment accounted for by expatriates in each cell of the sector/occupation matrix for the eight labor-importing countries grouped together in 1975. That table also reveals substantial disparities of expatriate shares among the sectors within each occupational category. The data suggest that certain sectors are especially successful or unsuccessful in attracting nationals, regardless of occupational level. This, conversely, affects the incidence of expatriates. This may be seen in Table 13, which displays the unweighted eight country average representation indexes among the sectors for each of the seven occupational categories. In that table sectors and occupations are arrayed from

**Table 12**

Expatriate Workers' Shares in Total Employment in the Eight
Major Labor-Importing Countries, by Sector, by Occupation, 1975

| Sector/Occupation | A-1 Professional-Technical Occupations | A-2 Other Professional Occupations | B-1 Technician Occupations | B-2 Other Subprofessional Occupations | C-1 Skilled Office & Manual Occupations | C-2 Semiskilled Office & Manual Occupations | D Unskilled Occupations | Total |
|---|---|---|---|---|---|---|---|---|
| Agriculture | 20.7 | 24.4 | 14.7 | 3.1 | 20.5 | 8.3 | 4.6 | 6.5 |
| Mining & Quarrying | 73.7 | 63.4 | 51.2 | 29.2 | 32.4 | 10.5 | 30.1 | 28.2 |
| Manufacturing | 51.2 | 53.0 | 26.6 | 31.9 | 62.9 | 14.0 | 16.4 | 26.1 |
| Utilities | 87.3 | 55.7 | 82.7 | 62.0 | 39.6 | 21.4 | 50.1 | 41.7 |
| Construction | 91.2 | 88.4 | 82.7 | 39.4 | 64.3 | 54.6 | 59.5 | 62.2 |
| Trade & Finance | 78.9 | 48.3 | 64.8 | 30.9 | 63.2 | 44.1 | 14.2 | 40.9 |
| Transportation & Communications | 80.8 | 63.2 | 49.6 | 55.4 | 29.2 | 34.2 | 38.5 | 38.0 |
| Services | 34.7 | 45.0 | 24.4 | 20.2 | 27.5 | 38.7 | 13.7 | 26.8 |
| Total | 61.8 | 53.6 | 40.3 | 22.2 | 46.1 | 26.9 | 15.7 | 26.8 |

**Table 13**

Unweighted Average Representation Indexes of Eight
Labor-Importing Countries among Sectors, by Occupations, 1975

| Sector/Occupation | B–2 Other Subprofessional Occupations | C–2 Semiskilled Office & Manual Occupations | C–1 Skilled Office and Manual Occupations | D Unskilled Occupations | A–2 Other Professional Occupations | B–2 Technician Occupations | A–1 Professional-Technical Occupations | Total |
|---|---|---|---|---|---|---|---|---|
| Agriculture | 1.13 | 1.30 | 1.42 | 1.71 | 2.07 | 1.82 | 2.07 | 1.69 |
| Services | 1.12 | 1.26 | 1.44 | 1.41 | 1.09 | 1.46 | 1.87 | 1.29 |
| Transportation & Communications | 0.71 | 1.10 | 1.24 | 1.22 | 1.19 | 1.53 | 0.96 | 1.13 |
| Utilities | 0.63 | 1.12 | 1.13 | 1.16 | 1.13 | 0.59 | 0.76 | 1.11 |
| Mining & Quarrying | 1.10 | 1.19 | 1.16 | 1.22 | 0.76 | 1.14 | 0.99 | 1.02 |
| Trade & Finance | 0.68 | 0.72 | 0.83 | 0.66 | 0.72 | 0.56 | 0.97 | 0.57 |
| Manufacturing | 0.64 | 0.55 | 0.57 | 0.83 | 0.91 | 0.83 | 0.97 | 0.57 |
| Construction | 0.41 | 0.46 | 0.48 | 0.44 | 0.49 | 0.34 | 0.32 | 0.45 |
| Total | 1.00 | 1.00 | 1.00 | 1.00 | 1.00 | 1.00 | 1.00 | 1.00 |
| (Specific Occupation Category Relative to Total Occupations) | (1.16) | (1.11) | (1.09) | (0.94) | (0.93) | (0.65) | (0.47) | (1.00) |

highest to lowest, top to bottom and left to right respectively. Agriculture and Services have consistent overrepresentation of nationals in all occupational categories, while construction, manufacturing and trade and finance show consistent underrepresentation of nationals across all occupational categories.

IV. Economic Implications for
the Labor-Importing Countries

The nature of the demand for immigrant labor in the Middle East differs considerably from that in Europe or elsewhere. First, the demand is not concentrated in a specific skill group (unskilled and semiskilled workers in Europe) or a sector (mining in South Africa), but it cuts across all sectors and skill levels and includes a sizable demand for highly skilled professionals and administrators. Secondly, the extent of reliance upon expatriate labor in the Middle Eastern labor-importing states is substantially greater.

In the Middle East, the labor-importing states' perspective on labor migration, and their motives for allowing or encouraging it, were profoundly different from the European or South African cases. The limited endowment of indigenous human capital relative to the financial resources of the oil-exporting states meant that, once economic growth had begun, there were no viable alternatives to labor imports, at least in the short-run. Self-sufficiency in labor would have meant only marginal increases in domestic investment and growth with large capital surpluses. This was unacceptable in a period of rapidly rising expectations.

Since 1974, it is labor imports which have enabled the oil-exporting countries to invest heavily, especially in infrastructure, to implement ambitious development programs. After six years of extensive labor imports, however, the necessity of keeping the expatriate population at a tolerable scale (with minimum political and cultural impact on the indigenous population) has once again made labor inputs the primary constraint on further accelerated economic growth. It is now becoming clear that future policies directed towards decreased dependence upon expatriate labor or increased investment beyond current levels will have to aim at more effective use of local labor supplies.

In most oil-exporting countries, there is certainly scope for increasing local labor supplies, both through increased labor participation and educational output. Crude labor force participation rates of nationals hover around 19 percent in major labor-importing countries, while female-participation rates are rarely over 10 percent. These rates are substantially lower than the average for the Middle East region (40 percent overall and 29 percent for females).[5] In the case of males, the demographic structure of these populations is largely the cause of the relatively low rate—most male members of the numerically small economically active age groups do participate in the economy, although because of their low educational attainment, they might not be active in either the sectors or at the occupational levels that the governments might desire.

In contrast, cultural constraints have generally caused employment of less well-educated women to be limited to family agricultural work and the traditional sector. Ironically, these traditional-sector employment opportunities for women are being eroded in most oil-exporting states by the expansion of the modern sector, where participation of women of low educational attainment is particularly limited. However, the way to expanding the female role in the modern sector of the oil-exporting states is through education. For females with secondary and higher education, labor force participation rates in the region, including the labor-importing countries, are strikingly high (in the 60–80 percent range). As the education systems continue to expand and improve in efficiency, the importance of females in the labor force will increase.

Relatively long lags are inherent, however, between internal and external education system improvements and the realization of the benefits of those improvements in terms of labor force impact. This, coupled with the small indigenous population bases of most labor-importing countries, will continue to cause heavy reliance upon expatriate manpower.

As the duration of reliance upon foreign workers has lengthened, the dependency rates of expatriate populations have increased. For certain expatriate nationalities, nearly normal population profiles already obtain in labor-importing countries. As a consequence of this demographic evolution of expatriate communities, the requirements for infrastructure and social services to support the nonnational populations have increased. These rising financial costs, and, more importantly, increased concern with nonnational-national population ratios, have led to increasingly close consideration by authorities in labor-importing countries of the trade-offs of economic growth and foreign labor requirements.

The most visible evidence of this concern is the increased reliance upon Korean construction firms which bring an entire work force, provide worker housing, live apart, and leave upon completion of the construction project. In addition to cost advantages, the social cost mini-

5. International Labor Office, *Labor Force Estimates and Projections 1950–2000, World Summary*, Vol. V, 1977.

**Table 14**

Manpower Requirements for the Major Labor-Importing Countries
by Year, 1975–1985

| | 1975 | 1976 | 1977 | 1978 | 1979 | 1980 |
|---|---|---|---|---|---|---|
| Total Manpower Requirement | 6,210,800 | 6,665,200 | 7,037,000 | 7,431,000 | 7,773,800 | 8,251,900 |
| Index | 100.0 | 107.3 | 113.3 | 119.6 | 125.2 | 132.9 |

| | 1981 | 1982 | 1983 | 1984 | 1985 | Net Growth 1975–1985 |
|---|---|---|---|---|---|---|
| Total Manpower Requirement | 8,658,300 | 9,015,600 | 9,368,600 | 9,794,300 | 10,306,600 | 4,095,800 |
| Index | 139.4 | 145.2 | 150.8 | 157.7 | 165.9 | |

mization of this approach is especially attractive to the labor-importing countries. There is also evidence that, in project selection, the labor-importing countries are now exercising increasing caution in proceeding with industrial developments necessitating substantial foreign labor importation.

In short, growing preoccupation with the national composition of the populations of the oil-exporting countries is becoming a new factor in tempering their rate of economic expansion. In projecting labor flows over the next decade, careful account will have to be taken of political factors which, through population policies, will have considerable influence upon both the scale and the nature of future migrant flows.

## B. Prospects for Future Labor Migration to the Capital-Rich States

### V. Introduction

Manpower requirements and supply projections have been carried out for the eight labor-importing countries using a computer model developed by the Technical Assistance and Special Studies Division of the Europe, Middle East and North Africa Region of the World Bank. This manpower forecasting model (Compound Model) consists of four submodels: Labor Force Submodel, Manpower Requirements Submodel, Education Simulation Submodel and the Manpower Policy Submodel.

### VI. Projected Total Manpower Requirements of the Eight Major Labor-Importing States

Over the 1975–1985 period, the total manpower requirements of the Labor Importing States of Algeria, Bahrain, Kuwait, Libya, Oman, Qatar, Saudi Arabia and UAE are projected to increase by over 4 million from about 6.2 million in 1975 to approximately 10.3 million in 1985 (Table 14). Their total manpower requirements in 1985 are projected to be nearly two-thirds as large again as in 1975. The relative growth of manpower demand is illustrated by the indexed growth to 165.9 in 1985 (1975=100). The sectoral composition of total manpower requirements are presented in Table 15. It shows that for the eight labor-importing countries, agricultural employment is projected by 1985 to have increased by only about 20 percent. Manufacturing is projected to realize the largest relative growth (1975 index of 100.0; 1985=230.7), followed by utilities (1985=

## Table 15

### Sectoral Composition and Growth of Total Manpower Requirements in the Eight Major Labor-Importing Countries, 1975, 1980 and 1985

| | 1975 | | 1980 | | 1985 | | Net Growth 1975–1985 | |
|---|---|---|---|---|---|---|---|---|
| | No. | % | No. | % | No. | % | No. | % |
| Agriculture | 2,297,900 | 37.0 | 2,411,900 | 29.2 | 2,760,200 | 26.8 | 462,300 | 11.3 |
| Index | 100.0 | | 105.0 | | 120.1 | | | |
| Mining & Quarrying | 115,100 | 1.9 | 179,200 | 2.2 | 211,300 | 2.1 | 96,200 | 2.3 |
| Index | 100.0 | | 155.6 | | 183.6 | | | |
| Manufacturing | 399,200 | 6.4 | 612,200 | 7.4 | 920,800 | 8.9 | 521,600 | 12.7 |
| Index | 100.0 | | 153.4 | | 206.8 | | | |
| Utilities | 62,700 | 1.0 | 92,300 | 1.1 | 129,700 | 1.3 | 67,000 | 1.6 |
| Index | 100.0 | | 147.1 | | 206.8 | | | |
| Construction | 946,100 | 15.2 | 1,463,600 | 17.7 | 1,633,500 | 15.8 | 687,400 | 16.8 |
| Index | 100.0 | | 154.7 | | 172.7 | | | |
| Trade & Finance | 613,500 | 9.9 | 937,200 | 11.4 | 1,210,600 | 11.7 | 597,100 | 14.6 |
| Index | 100.0 | | 152.8 | | 197.3 | | | |
| Transport & Communications | 312,300 | 5.0 | 505,800 | 6.1 | 579,200 | 5.6 | 266,800 | 6.5 |
| Index | 100.0 | | 161.9 | | 185.4 | | | |
| Services | 1,464,000 | 23.6 | 2,049,900 | 24.8 | 2,861,300 | 27.8 | 1,397,300 | 34.1 |
| Index | 100.0 | | 140.0 | | 195.4 | | | |
| Total | 6,210,800 | 100.0 | 8,251,900 | 100.0 | 10,306,600 | 100.0 | 4,095,700 | 100.0 |
| | 100.0 | | 132.9 | | 165.9 | | | |

206.8), trade and finance (1985=197.3), and services (1985=195.4). In terms of volume, over a third of the net increase is projected as accruing to the services sectors. Other major increases are accounted for by construction (17 percent), trade and finance (15 percent) and manufacturing (13 percent). Features of the projected changing structural composition of manpower requirements in the 1975–1985 period of special interest are the decline in the share of agriculture (from 37.0 percent in 1975 to 27 percent in 1985), and the increased shares of manufacturing (from 6 percent in 1975 to 9 percent in 1985) and of services (from 24 percent in 1975 to 28 percent in 1985).

The occupational composition of manpower requirements is projected to change rapidly and substantially over the 1975–1985 period. Table 16 shows that for the eight states in question, the unskilled occupations' share of employment is projected to fall from 44 percent in 1975 to 39 percent in 1985. Semiskilled occupations are projected as declining from 28 percent in 1975 to 26 percent in 1985. All other occupations show a steadily increasing share over the projection period.

The relative growth of the various occupation groups is most easily seen by examination of the indexes of occupational growth (1975=100.0). By 1985 the index for professional-technical occupations is projected as 270.0, followed by technician occupations (250.4),and other professional occupations (225.2). The slowest relative growth is projected for unskilled occupations (147.8) and semiskilled office and manual occupations (153.3). Despite their relatively slow growth, the latter two occupations are nonetheless projected as accounting for a majority of net growth of manpower requirements during the 1975–1985 period.

## VII. Projected Supply of Nationals of the Labor-Importing States to the Labor Force from the Domestic Educational/Training Systems

The volume and education/training qualifications of future national entrants to the labor force were projected in the Education Simulation submodel of the Compound Model. Individuals who never enter school as well as school entrants were taken into account in the course of the application of this submodel. Table 17 summarizes for the labor-importing countries the total flows of nationals from their education/training systems as matched with occupational categories. The table shows substantial improvements in the qualitative profile of national labor force entrants between the 1976–1980 and 1981–85 periods. Nevertheless, the Arab labor-importing countries are unlikely to be able to expand and im-

**Table 16**

Occupational Composition and Growth of Total Manpower Requirements
in the Eight Major Labor-Importing Countries, 1975, 1980 and 1985

| | 1975 | | 1980 | | 1985 | | Net Growth 1975–1985 | |
|---|---|---|---|---|---|---|---|---|
| | No. | % | No. | % | No. | % | No. | % |
| **A–1: Professional-Technical** | | | | | | | | |
| Occupations | 110,000 | 1.8 | 202,600 | 2.5 | 297,300 | 2.9 | 187,200 | 4.6 |
| Index | 100.0 | | 184.1 | | 270.0 | | | |
| **A–2: Other Professional** | | | | | | | | |
| Occupations | 250,100 | 4.0 | 399,600 | 4.8 | 563,400 | 5.5 | 313,300 | 7.6 |
| Index | 100.0 | | 159.7 | | 225.2 | | | |
| **B–1: Technician Occupations** | 190,400 | 3.1 | 334,300 | 4.1 | 476,700 | 4.6 | 286,300 | 7.0 |
| Index | 100.0 | | 175.6 | | 250.4 | | | |
| **B–2: Other Subprofessional** | | | | | | | | |
| Occupations | 249,700 | 4.0 | 361,500 | 4.4 | 490,100 | 4.8 | 240,400 | 5.9 |
| Index | 100.0 | | 144.8 | | 196.3 | | | |
| **C–1: Skilled Office &** | | | | | | | | |
| Manual Occupations | 923,400 | 14.9 | 1,353,100 | 16.4 | 1,750,200 | 17.0 | 826,800 | 20.2 |
| Index | 100.0 | | 146.5 | | 189.5 | | | |
| **C–2: Semiskilled Office** | | | | | | | | |
| & Manual Occupations | 1,752,100 | 28.2 | 2,077,600 | 25.2 | 2,685,900 | 26.1 | 933,800 | 22.8 |
| Index | 100.0 | | 118.6 | | 153.3 | | | |
| **D: Unskilled Occupations** | 2,735,000 | 44.0 | 3,523,300 | 42.7 | 4,043,000 | 39.2 | 1,307,900 | 31.9 |
| Index | 100.0 | | 128.8 | | 147.8 | | | |
| **Total** | 6,210,800 | 100.0 | 8,251,900 | 100.0 | 10,306,600 | 100.0 | 4,095,700 | 100.0 |
| Index | 100.0 | | 132.9 | | 165.9 | | | |

## Table 17

Projected Average Annual Education/Training System Supplies in the Eight Labor-Importing States for Occupations for Periods 1976–80 and 1980–85

| Period | Occupation | A–1 Professional-Technical Occupation | A–2 Other Professional Occupation | B–1 Technical Occupation | B–2 Other Sub-professional Occupation | C–1 Skilled Office & Manual Occupation | C–2 Semiskilled Office Occupation | D Unskilled Occupation | Total |
|---|---|---|---|---|---|---|---|---|---|
| 1976–80 | Number | 4,100 | 8,900 | 4,700 | 14,200 | 20,050 | 80,800 | 239,050 | 371,800 |
| | % | 1.10 | 2.39 | 1.26 | 3.82 | 5.39 | 21.73 | 64.31 | 100% |
| 1981–85 | Number | 8,000 | 13,900 | 8,750 | 24,300 | 36,800 | 136,050 | 232,700 | 460,500 |
| | % | 1.74 | 3.02 | 1.90 | 5.28 | 7.99 | 29.54 | 50.53 | 100% |

## Table 18

Comparison of Projected Net Growth of Manpower
Requirements 1976–85 with Supply of Nationals Entering Labor
Force 1976–85, for Eight Major Labor-Importing Countries

| Occupation | Net Growth in Manpower Requirements 1975–85 | | National Labor Force Entrants 1976–85 | | Supply as % of Requirements |
|---|---|---|---|---|---|
| | No. | % | No. | % | |
| A–1: Professional-Technical Occupations | 187,200 | 4.6 | 60,400 | 1.5 | 32.2 |
| A–2: Other Professional Occupations | 313,300 | 7.6 | 114,500 | 2.8 | 36.5 |
| B–1: Technician Occupations | 286,300 | 7.0 | 67,400 | 4.6 | 79.9 |
| B–2: Other Subprofessional Occupations | 240,400 | 5.9 | 192,100 | 4.6 | 79.9 |
| C–1: Skilled Office & Manual Occupations | 826,800 | 20.2 | 284,700 | 6.8 | 34.4 |
| C–2: Semiskilled Office & Manual Occupations | 933,800 | 22.8 | 1,084,100 | 26.0 | 116.1 |
| D: Unskilled Occupations | 1,037,900 | 31.9 | 2,358,700 | 56.7 | 227.3 |
| Total | 4,095,700 | 100.0 | 4,161,800 | 100.0 | 101.6 |

prove the internal and external efficiencies of their educational/training system with sufficient speed to avoid continued and increased reliance upon imported nonnational manpower.

Table 18 illustrates this by comparing the net growth of manpower requirements in the Arab labor-importing countries between 1975 and 1985 with comparable education training systems outputs for the period 1976–1985. The requirements figures ignore the demand due to attrition of nationals already in the labor force and excludes the quantity of jobs held by expatriates in 1975. Even with these demand factors omitted, the supply of nationals during the projection period will fall far short of requirements in the professional, technical and skilled worker categories of occupations. Only in unskilled and semi-skilled occupational categories will there be a potential for reduced reliance on or replacement of expatriates. Those figures also suggest a major difficulty confronting human resources development authorities in the labor-importing countries. Very large proportions of labor force entrants have little, if any, education. Consequently, literacy and numeracy deficiencies of potential trainees must be taken seriously into account if training programs are to be effectively implemented.

Of the eight labor-importing countries under study, in no case is the projected supply of nationals sufficient to fill all occupational categories of the country's manpower requirements within the projection horizon. Projections for most states show their nationals' share of employment as steadily falling, or, at best, fluctuating at levels only occasionally slightly higher, and generally lower, than the 1975 level.

Overall by 1985, expatriates are projected to comprise some 35 percent of employment in the eight labor-importing states. No surpluses of nationals in any occupational category in any year are projected for a majority of the oil-exporting states. In a couple of instances small surpluses of unskilled workers are projected for the late 1980s. Similar surpluses of other subprofessionals sometimes occur but such workers could quite likely find employment in skilled office and manual occupations where shortages remain acute. Nationals in this (skilled office and manual) occupational category are projected to be sufficient to supply only a share of employment declining from 54 percent in 1976 to 25 percent in 1985.

## VIII. The Nonnational Labor Requirements in Detail

Over the 1975–1985 period, the nonnational manpower requirements of the eight Middle East and North African labor-importing countries under study are projected to more than double, to 3.6 million between 1975 and

## Table 19

### Growth of Total Expatriate Manpower Requirements in the Eight Major Labor-Importing Countries 1975–1985

| | 1975 | 1976 | 1977 | 1978 | 1979 | 1980 | 1981 | 1982 | 1983 | 1984 | 1985 | Net Growth (1975–1985) |
|---|---|---|---|---|---|---|---|---|---|---|---|---|
| Total | 1,661,200 | 1,929,000 | 2,112,000 | 2,267,400 | 2,458,000 | 2,658,000 | 2,832,400 | 2,989,400 | 3,154,600 | 3,370,800 | 3,616,100 | 1,954,900 |
| | 100.0 | 116.1 | 127.1 | 136.5 | 148.0 | 160.0 | 170.5 | 180.0 | 189.9 | 202.9 | 217.7 | |
| Incremental Growth | | 267,800 | 183,000 | 155,400 | 191,000 | 199,600 | 174,400 | 157,000 | 165,200 | 216,200 | 245,300 | |
| Incremental Growth Rate | | 16.1% | 9.5% | 7.4% | 8.4% | 8.1% | 6.6% | 5.5% | 5.5% | 6.9% | 7.3% | |

1985 (Table 19). The volume of expatriate manpower required is projected to increase in each country, each year through 1985. The net growth in expatriate manpower requirements in the eight major Arab labor-importing countries over the 1975–1985 period is projected at just under 2 million. Relative to the 1975 base year, the projected increase in expatriate requirements amounts to 217.7 (1975 index of 100.0).

In terms of the occupational composition requirements, by 1985, expatriate manpower requirements to the technician occupations are projected to more than quadruple, and for the professional-technical occupations to more than triple in comparison with their respective 1975 levels. Only in the unskilled and semiskilled office and manual occupations are requirements for 1985 projected to be less than double their 1975 levels. These latter two occupational categories are projected to account together for just under one-quarter of net additional expatriate manpower requirements for the 1975–1985 period. Technical and other professional occupational groups together are shown to account for about 20 percent, the technician (science based) occupational group for 13 percent, and the skilled office and manual occupational groups for 36 percent of the net growth of expatriate requirements over the projection period. Tables 20 and 21 show the occupational composition and its evolution for the Arab labor-importing countries.

This projected evolution to a more highly skilled and educated profile of expatriate manpower will have significant consequences for the labor-supplying countries. More than ever, the demand for manpower is likely to drain the labor-exporting countries of their better-qualified workers. Already, in 1975, high proportions of vacancies in professional, technical and clerical occupations in the labor importers were constrained by a requirement of Arabic and English language competence. Consequently, it is reasonable to assume that high- and middle-level manpower in Arab labor-exporting countries will be increasingly sought after by public and private employers in the labor-importing countries. The wider recruiting areas of South and South East Asia, which have supplied increasingly large shares of additional expatriate manpower since the mid 1970s, may not be so appropriate as sources of labor in the future as the structure of expatriate manpower requirements shifts from unskilled and semiskilled production and service occupations to more highly skilled and professional occupations. Non-Arab labor, however, may well play an increasingly important role in sectors and occupations for which Arabic language facility is not an important consideration.

It is also possible that the labor-importing countries will find means of structuring employment situations in manufacturing and other sectors

## Table 20

### Number and Relative Growth of Expatriate Manpower Requirements in the Eight Major Labor-Importing Countries, by Occupation 1975–1980

| | 1975 | 1976 | 1977 | 1978 | 1979 | 1980 | 1981 | 1982 | 1983 | 1984 | 1985 | Net Growth 1975–85 |
|---|---|---|---|---|---|---|---|---|---|---|---|---|
| A–1 Professional-Technical | 67,900 | 96,400 | 107,900 | 118,700 | 130,500 | 145,400 | 155,800 | 166,000 | 177,700 | 191,100 | 214,600 | 146,700 |
| Index | 100.0 | 142.0 | 158.9 | 174.8 | 192.2 | 214.2 | 229.5 | 244.5 | 261.7 | 281.4 | 316.1 | |
| A–2 Other Professional | 134,000 | 165,100 | 185,700 | 207,400 | 229,300 | 255,900 | 275,200 | 295,600 | 317,400 | 340,000 | 378,800 | 244,800 |
| Index | 100.0 | 123.2 | 138.6 | 154.8 | 171.1 | 191.0 | 205.4 | 220.6 | 236.9 | 253.7 | 282.7 | |
| B–1 Technician (Science Based) | 76,800 | 126,100 | 145,700 | 162,100 | 182,500 | 211,100 | 233,300 | 251,500 | 268,000 | 289,900 | 325,000 | 248,600 |
| Index | 100.0 | 164.5 | 190.0 | 211.5 | 238.0 | 275.4 | 304.5 | 328.0 | 349.7 | 378.2 | 424.6 | |
| B–2 Other Subprofessional | 55,400 | 70,500 | 85,500 | 100,100 | 110,200 | 124,000 | 135,100 | 141,700 | 145,700 | 152,700 | 166,000 | 110,600 |
| Index | 100.0 | 127.3 | 154.3 | 180.7 | 180.9 | 223.8 | 243.9 | 255.8 | 263.0 | 275.6 | 299.6 | |
| C–1 Skilled Office & Manual | 425,800 | 524,300 | 597,400 | 669,100 | 751,900 | 822,700 | 875,200 | 923,500 | 972,000 | 1,028,500 | 1,111,200 | 685,400 |
| Index | 100.0 | 123.1 | 140.3 | 157.1 | 176.6 | 193.2 | 205.5 | 216.9 | 228.3 | 241.5 | 261.0 | |
| C–2 Semiskilled Office & Manual | 471,600 | 464,400 | 503,700 | 530,700 | 566,100 | 606,900 | 657,100 | 704,800 | 759,800 | 827,800 | 869,800 | 398,200 |
| Index | 100.0 | 98.5 | 106.8 | 112.5 | 120.0 | 128.7 | 139.3 | 149.4 | 161.1 | 175.5 | 184.4 | |
| D Unskilled | 429,700 | 482,200 | 486,100 | 479,300 | 487,900 | 492,000 | 500,700 | 506,300 | 513,900 | 540,800 | 550,300 | 120,600 |
| Index | 100.0 | 112.2 | 113.1 | 111.5 | 113.5 | 114.5 | 116.5 | 117.8 | 119.6 | 125.9 | 128.1 | |
| Total all occupations | 1,661,200 | 1,929,000 | 2,112,000 | 2,267,400 | 2,458,400 | 2,658,400 | 2,832,400 | 2,989,400 | 3,154,600 | 3,370,800 | 3,616,100 | 1,954,900 |
| Index | 100.0 | 116.1 | 127.1 | 136.5 | 148.0 | 160.0 | 170.5 | 180.0 | 189.9 | 202.9 | 217.7 | |

**Table 21**

Percentage Distribution among Occupations of Expatriate Manpower Requirements in the Eight Labor-Importing Countries, 1975–1985

| Occupation | 1975 | 1976 | 1977 | 1978 | 1979 | 1980 | 1981 | 1982 | 1983 | 1984 | 1985 | Net Growth 1975–85 |
|---|---|---|---|---|---|---|---|---|---|---|---|---|
| A–1 Professional-Technical | 4.1 | 5.0 | 5.1 | 5.2 | 5.3 | 5.5 | 5.5 | 5.6 | 5.6 | 5.7 | 5.9 | 7.5 |
| A–2 Other Professional | 8.1 | 8.6 | 8.8 | 9.2 | 9.3 | 9.6 | 9.7 | 9.9 | 10.1 | 10.1 | 10.5 | 12.5 |
| B–1 Technician (Science Based) | 4.6 | 6.5 | 6.9 | 7.2 | 7.4 | 7.9 | 8.2 | 8.4 | 8.5 | 8.6 | 9.0 | 12.7 |
| B–2 Other Subprofessional | 3.3 | 3.7 | 4.0 | 4.4 | 4.5 | 4.7 | 4.8 | 4.7 | 4.6 | 4.5 | 4.6 | 5.7 |
| C–1 Skilled Office & Manual | 25.6 | 27.2 | 28.3 | 29.5 | 30.6 | 31.0 | 30.9 | 30.9 | 30.8 | 30.5 | 30.7 | 35.1 |
| C–2 Semiskilled Office & Manual | 28.4 | 24.1 | 23.8 | 23.4 | 23.0 | 22.8 | 23.2 | 23.6 | 24.1 | 24.6 | 24.1 | 20.4 |
| D  Unskilled | 25.9 | 25.0 | 23.0 | 21.1 | 19.9 | 18.5 | 17.7 | 16.9 | 16.3 | 16.0 | 15.2 | 6.2 |
| Total all occupations | 100.0 | 100.0 | 100.0 | 100.0 | 100.0 | 100.0 | 100.0 | 100.0 | 100.0 | 100.0 | 100.0 | 100.0 |

## Table 22

Expatriate Manpower Requirements as Percentage
of Total Manpower Requirements in Eight Major Labor-
Importing Countries, 1975, 1980 and 1985

| | A-1 Professional-Technical Occupations | A-2 Other Professional Occupations | B-1 Technician Occupations | B-2 Other Sub-professional Occupations | C-1 Skilled Office & Manual Occupations | C-2 Semiskilled Office & Manual Occupations | D Unskilled Occupations | Total |
|---|---|---|---|---|---|---|---|---|
| 1975 | 61.8 | 53.6 | 40.4 | 22.2 | 46.1 | 26.9 | 15.7 | 26.7 |
| 1980 | 71.8 | 64.1 | 63.2 | 34.3 | 60.8 | 29.2 | 14.0 | 32.2 |
| 1985 | 72.2 | 67.2 | 68.4 | 33.9 | 63.5 | 32.4 | 13.6 | 35.1 |

similar to the approach used in the construction sector (e.g. Korean contractors' self-contained projects) and in ports operation whereby the entire labor force for a project is imported as a package. Specific projects in the industrial estates currently under development will rely upon imported labor-force "packages" for initial operation as well as construction. Militating against long-term reliance upon imported-labor "packages" for plant operation, however, is the desire of national authorities to have a high incidence of nationals employed in such highly visible and symbolic efforts in economic diversification.

The sectoral composition of projected nonnational requirements are, at this stage, less firm than projections of occupational composition. In addition to an oversimplified presumption of the homogeneity of manpower within each occupational category, sectoral preference patterns of nationals in the labor-importing countries have been deliberately ignored at this stage. It is with the above caveats in mind that projected expatriate manpower requirements' sectoral composition should be read.

Table 23 shows the projected expatriate requirements of the eight labor-importing states by sector. The most rapid and largest growth occurs in the services sector, which by 1985 will absorb more than one-third of the imported workers in these states (Table 24).

## Conclusion

Overall, nonnational workers in the Arab labor-importing countries accounted for 26.7 percent of their total labor force in 1975. By 1980 their overall share is projected to have risen to 32.2 percent and to reach 35.1 percent by 1985.

By 1985 nearly three-quarters of professional-technical jobs and about two-thirds of other professional, technical, and skilled office and manual jobs are projected to require expatriate workers. Only in unskilled jobs is the expatriate share projected to decline, from about 16 percent in 1975 to just under 14 percent in 1985. The pattern is set for increased reliance on expatriate workers in the labor-importing states.

This is especially the case at the higher-occupational levels, where there are already signs of a regional shortage of labor. Despite significantly expanded education system enrollments and outputs of nationals within the labor-importing countries over the projection period, the labor-importing countries are projected to be increasingly reliant upon expatriates to fill high- and middle-level manpower positions. By 1985 over three-fourths of professional-technical and two-thirds of other professional, technician and skilled office and manual jobs will require expatri-

**Table 23**

Number and Relative Growth of Expatriate Manpower Requirements in Labor-Importing Countries by Sector

| Sector | 1975 | 1976 | 1977 | 1978 | 1979 | 1980 | 1981 | 1982 | 1983 | 1984 | 1985 | Net Growth 1975–85 |
|---|---|---|---|---|---|---|---|---|---|---|---|---|
| Agriculture | 148,400 | 162,000 | 164,100 | 164,800 | 167,400 | 210,500 | 251,700 | 295,100 | 334,400 | 377,500 | 419,500 | 271,100 |
| Index | 100.0 | 109.2 | 110.5 | 111.1 | 112.8 | 141.8 | 169.7 | 198.9 | 225.3 | 254.4 | 282.7 | |
| Mining & Quarrying | 32,500 | 35,300 | 45,900 | 48,400 | 50,700 | 54,000 | 56,000 | 58,000 | 59,400 | 61,200 | 63,500 | 31,000 |
| Index | 100.0 | 108.6 | 141.2 | 148.9 | 156.0 | 166.2 | 172.3 | 178.5 | 182.8 | 188.3 | 195.4 | |
| Manufacturing | 104,400 | 120,700 | 136,800 | 144,400 | 152,300 | 165,900 | 182,300 | 200,000 | 220,100 | 246,100 | 272,400 | 168,000 |
| Index | 100.0 | 115.6 | 131.0 | 138.3 | 145.9 | 158.9 | 174.6 | 191.6 | 210.8 | 235.7 | 260.9 | |
| Utilities | 26,200 | 29,300 | 33,700 | 38,100 | 42,300 | 46,800 | 51,300 | 55,800 | 60,200 | 65,500 | 70,800 | 44,600 |
| Index | 100.0 | 112.0 | 128.6 | 145.8 | 161.7 | 178.9 | 195.7 | 213.0 | 230.5 | 250.0 | 270.9 | |
| Construction | 588,200 | 636,300 | 668,200 | 696,300 | 756,800 | 794,200 | 804,400 | 794,400 | 795,800 | 813,300 | 851,300 | 263,100 |
| Index | 100.0 | 108.2 | 113.6 | 118.4 | 128.7 | 135.0 | 136.8 | 135.1 | 135.3 | 138.3 | 144.7 | |
| Trade & Finance | 250,900 | 297,000 | 313,600 | 333,100 | 352,200 | 368,100 | 384,400 | 400,600 | 417,900 | 439,000 | 461,800 | 210,900 |
| Index | 100.0 | 118.4 | 125.0 | 132.8 | 140.4 | 146.7 | 153.2 | 159.7 | 166.6 | 175.0 | 184.1 | |
| Transportation & Communications | 118,900 | 154,300 | 176,800 | 204,300 | 236,800 | 234,200 | 235,300 | 237,100 | 239,800 | 243,300 | 244,800 | 125,000 |
| Index | 100.0 | 129.7 | 148.7 | 171.8 | 199.2 | 197.0 | 197.9 | 199.4 | 201.7 | 204.6 | 205.9 | |
| Services | 391,700 | 494,100 | 572,900 | 638,000 | 699,800 | 784,300 | 867,000 | 948,400 | 1,027,000 | 1,124,900 | 1,232,000 | 840,300 |
| Index | 100.0 | 126.1 | 146.3 | 162.9 | 178.7 | 200.2 | 221.3 | 242.1 | 262.2 | 287.2 | 314.5 | |
| Total | 1,661,200 | 1,929,000 | 2,112,000 | 2,267,400 | 2,458,400 | 2,658,000 | 2,832,400 | 2,989,400 | 3,154,600 | 3,370,800 | 3,616,100 | 1,954,900 |

**Table 24**

Percentage Distribution among Sectors of Expatriate
Manpower Requirements in the Eight Importing Countries
1975–1985

| Sector | 1975 | 1976 | 1977 | 1978 | 1979 | 1980 | 1981 | 1982 | 1983 | 1984 | 1985 | Net Growth 1975–85 |
|---|---|---|---|---|---|---|---|---|---|---|---|---|
| Agriculture | 8.9 | 8.4 | 7.8 | 7.3 | 6.8 | 7.9 | 8.9 | 9.9 | 10.6 | 11.2 | 11.6 | 13.8 |
| Mining & Quarrying | 2.0 | 1.8 | 2.2 | 2.1 | 2.1 | 2.0 | 2.0 | 1.9 | 1.9 | 1.8 | 1.8 | 1.6 |
| Manufacturing | 6.3 | 6.3 | 6.5 | 6.4 | 6.2 | 6.2 | 6.4 | 6.7 | 7.0 | 7.3 | 7.5 | 8.6 |
| Utilities | 1.6 | 1.5 | 1.6 | 1.7 | 1.7 | 1.8 | 1.8 | 1.9 | 1.9 | 1.9 | 1.9 | 2.3 |
| Construction | 35.3 | 33.0 | 31.6 | 30.7 | 30.8 | 29.9 | 28.4 | 26.6 | 25.2 | 24.1 | 23.5 | 13.5 |
| Trade & Finance | 15.1 | 15.4 | 14.8 | 14.7 | 14.3 | 13.9 | 13.6 | 13.4 | 13.2 | 13.0 | 12.8 | 10.8 |
| Transportation & Communications | 7.2 | 8.0 | 8.4 | 9.0 | 9.6 | 8.8 | 8.3 | 7.9 | 7.6 | 7.2 | 6.8 | 6.4 |
| Services | 23.6 | 25.6 | 27.1 | 28.1 | 28.5 | 29.5 | 30.6 | 31.7 | 32.6 | 33.4 | 34.1 | 43.0 |
| Total | 100.0 | 100.0 | 100.0 | 100.0 | 100.0 | 100.0 | 100.0 | 100.0 | 100.0 | 100.0 | 100.0 | 100.0 |

ate manpower. It is at these occupational levels that competence in Arabic and English lanuage often becomes important. Consequently, the Arab labor-exporting countries will experience yet greater demand for their better-educated manpower from the oil-endowed states.

In 1975, Arab migrant workers comprised about 60 percent of the total number of expatriate workers in the labor-importing countries. Their share has fallen in subsequent years as labor recruitment agents from India and Pakistan have helped facilitate a rapid and large flow of workers to the oil-endowed countries to meet the manpower requirements generated by heightened economic activity following the post-1973 oil-price-increase boom.

Further formalization of international labor supplies to the oil-rich states resulted in rapid expansion in the share of expatriate workers accounted for by South East Asian labor. The Korean contractors who brought self-contained work crews to the rapidly expanding construction sector were the earliest example of this. The rapid growth in numbers of South East Asian workers is accounted for first by the boom in the construction sector (which accounted for 34 percent of expatriate requirements in 1975), and subsequently by the application of their style of contracting to other sectors in the oil-endowed states, as exemplified by the "packages" of labor imported for stevedoring and on-shore freight handling at the ports. Likewise, the large petro-chemical projects under development in the new industrial estates of the oil countries will be initially operated by packaged workforces provided by the joint venture partners—but in these cases, the plant workforces will be drawn from the industrially advanced home countries of the joint venture partners, e.g. Japan, Taiwan, the United States, and European countries.

The Korean contractor mode of operation, supplying a complete workforce, was particularly appealing to authorities in labor-importing countries who were becoming increasingly concerned with the social consequences of a large expatriate presence, and who were finding supplies of good quality labor difficult to recruit from more traditional sources.

Several key issues arise from this background of developments in recent years and from projected future requirements: as the construction phase of economic development in the oil countries begins to taper off and stabilize, the demand for huge quantities of unskilled and semiskilled labor will diminish relative to requirements for skilled, technician and professional workers. Whether for reasons of cost, convenience, or necessity, labor-importing countries have shifted, at least at the margin, to recruitment of South and South East Asian labor to meet their needs for workers. There could be substantial displacement of Arab migrant labor by workers from a wide variety of competing South, East and South East Asian countries, particularly if the People's Republic of China successfully follows through its announced plans to supply construction crews for the Middle East labor market.

At this same time, the numbers of unskilled and semiskilled nationals of oil-rich states entering the labor market will increase rapidly. Whether they will accept employment in the construction, manufacturing and personal services sectors (which in the past they appear to have shunned) remains to be seen. Certainly there are signs of caste attitudes setting in among nationals which result in a wide array of jobs being considered the preserve of nonnationals. Should these occupational avoidance-preference attitudes harden, the labor importing-countries may well have very serious problems of unemployment, or at least underemployment/disguised unemployment of nationals who choose not to work in those sectors and occupations most heavily reliant upon immigrant workers.

Unless extremely imaginative and extensive out-of-school education/training programs can be designed and implemented, the oil-endowed states will suffer the irony of seeing their domestic human capital underutilized at a time when they are growing increasingly concerned over labor imports.

For the Arab labor-exporting countries, the potential displacement of Arab migrant unskilled and semiskilled labor by non-Arab workers and the consequent possible net return home of erstwhile migrants presents a critical economic issue. These poor Arab states, grown accustomed to exporting labor, could be faced with the absorption of returning migrants just at the time their remittance receipts would be in decline and when, as a result, their ability to invest in job-creating programs is also falling.

However, the fact that Arabic language and cultural homogeneity preference constraints operate on the oil countries' requirements for high- and middle-level expatriate manpower means that the Arab labor-exporting countries will be increasingly drained of their more skilled and talented labor force members. It is precisely this type of out-migration which is least beneficial to labor-exporting countries. Although income levels of skilled professional migrants are high, such migrants usually are accompanied by dependents. Their remittance rates are generally much lower, therefore, than those of unaccompanied migrant workers. Furthermore, the loss of even small numbers of skilled, educated, and experienced workers can cause severe bottlenecks in production and development. This will serve to aggravate the inability of the economies of the labor supplying countries to grow, and hence to absorb the net return of unskilled workers.

Only by considering the Arab region as a whole, examining the simulated results of alternative scenarios, can appropriate assessment of the impact of international worker migration upon labor importers and exporters be understood and made clear.

# Policy Dilemmas for International Migration in the Middle East

## By Charles B. Keely

THE LARGE LABOR MIGRATIONS within and to the Middle East in the 1970s and those projected for the 1980s raise significant policy questions for the sending and receiving countries. Reviews of development prospects and labor-force data (including migration of foreign labor) require a review of some of these policy issues and of the examples of previous labor migrations which serve as implicit or explicit models for policy makers.

### Sending Countries

The issue of labor export is frequently presented as a mutually beneficial process for the sending and receiving countries. From the side of the sending country, the migration of labor is presented as an opportunity to export excess labor, thereby reducing the numbers of unemployed (and potential sources of political instability). Workers are seen as gaining valuable experience overseas, which can be applied to national development upon their return. Remittances from migrant workers are desirable for a variety of reasons: they increase foreign currency reserves, they help the balance of payments, and they provide investment capital for development with a concomitant increase in jobs.

These proposed benefits, however, are seen as being available within a buyers market. There are many sending countries, and potential workers are seen as legion. Sending countries are discouraged not only from collaborating to form any sort of "labor cartel" but also from collectively working to insure minimum standards of pay and conditions. Sending countries see themselves, to some extent, as competitors that must rely on market forces for export of workers to other countries, and on the goodwill and good sense of receiving countries to avoid outrageous treatment of workers.

As happened in the case of labor-exporting countries supplying European "guestworkers," Arab (and even South and East Asian) countries supplying labor to Middle East oil exporters are now questioning the mutually benefical scenario. Unemployed workers are usually not the ones who migrate. Often it is the skilled and experienced workers who are skimmed off a very thin layer of such a labor force. Replacement of these workers requires manpower training and time. The absence of experienced workers shows up not only in inconvenience to the sending country's middle and upper classes seeking skilled tradesmen, but also in labor bottlenecks and even the importation of foreign labor on domestic projects. Jordan is perhaps the quintessential example of this problem. With an estimated 30 plus percent of Jordan's labor force outside the country, Egyptian migrants work at construction sites in Amman, Korean companies and workers build houses and roads in the Jordan Valley, and Pakistani workers are found in Amman hotels. Although perhaps an extreme example, the Jordanian experience underlines the fact that the workers who go abroad are not the jobless (redundant labor, if you will). Sending countries are faced, therefore, with manpower development policy dilemmas. Training programs primarily may produce better-qualified candidates for foreign jobs in the short run. The lack of control over the demand for labor in receiving countries makes medium-term manpower planning hazardous since the sending country may face a large return of workers if development drops off in labor-importing countries for any of a variety of possible reasons.

The valuable experience supposedly gained by migrant workers may also prove illusory. The experience gained may not be transferable because of the kinds of technology used in the oil-rich states on various projects or, in fact, new skills may not be learned. The assumption that human capital investment, in the form of new experience and skills, is easily transferable to a different economic context (e.g., from Saudi Arabia to Yemen), represents hope rather than hard-nosed planning decisions.

Remittances are, of course, a major attraction for sending countries. Thus, labor-exporting countries want to maximize remittances and maximize their transfer through official channels so that the hard currency can be captured.

Remittances, however, are different from foreign investment or foreign aid. Unlike the latter, they are not earmarked for specific projects or readily available to goverments for direct investment.[1] Thus, while they are

1. Zafer H. Ecevit, "International Labor Migration in the Middle East and North Africa—Trends, Effects, and Policies." Paper presented at the Bellagio Conference on Interna-

useful for balance-of-trade and hard-currency purposes, one cannot presuppose remittances will be invested in economic development and job creation. Remittances may, in fact, finance increased food imports or imports to satisfy newly acquired tastes for consumer goods. They may also fuel inflation by distorting land prices, raising construction costs due to investment in new housing, and so on. Experience from instances of previous labor exporters (e.g., Turkish workers to Europe) is not comforting regarding the use of remittances. Rather than going into savings or investments, they are likely to be used for housing, land speculation, consumer durables, and small scale investments like shops and taxis. Governments need to develop incentives to pool remittances for large-scale investments with multiplier effects and job-creation potential beyond the examples given above. Few models are available for successful pooling of remittances through savings and investment schemes.

In addition, large influxes of remittances of money and goods are not always evenly distributed throughout the country. And there is a question as to whether the absence of workers and the remittance they send home encourage relocation to urban centers, thus furthering rural-urban income and investment imbalances.

In short, the mutually beneficial scenario is being questioned by Middle East labor suppliers, as European guestworker-supplying countries did earlier. It should be noted that data on worker flows, duration of stay, skill composition, and on amounts and actual use of remittances, are poor or virtually nonexistent. Nevertheless, the migration phenomenon takes place and policies exist, whether they are adopted actively or become de facto through inaction.

For Arab and nonregional labor suppliers from South and East Asia, the flow of workers affects manpower development plans and programs, timing of development projects, income distribution policy, import policy (e.g., food, consumer durables), and efforts to control wages and prices.[2] Since governments generally are reacting to the existence of migration, their major concern is to control it and maximize its benefits, as opposed to trying to adopt a policy to prohibit migration. Their efforts to control the flows are inhibited because they depend on the development policies of labor importers and these are often well beyond their ability to influ-

tional Migration, June 1979, p. 14. Forthcoming in M. Kritz, C. Keely, and S. Tomasi, eds., *Global Trends in Migration: Theory and Research on International Population Movements* (New York Center For Migration Studies, 1981).

2. Charles B. Keely, "Asian Worker Migration to the Middle East," Center for Policy Studies Working Paper No. 52, The Population Council, New York (January 1980).

ence, much less to control. The flow of remittances, while beneficial for balances of trade and foreign currency reserves, also puts labor exporters in a dependent position. This dependency may feed upon itself, in a sense, like drug dependency. Remittances are needed for food and other imports, requiring continued labor export, which may require even further remittances. At all times, it is the state of the economies and their development plans which control the availability of jobs and resulting remittances. A falling off of the demand for labor not only would reduce remittances but would mean a return of workers in numbers greater than the absorptive capacity of the economies of the sending countries.

## Receiving Countries

The development plans of oil exporting countries have required labor supplies well beyond the capacity of domestic resources. As Birks has pointed out in his presentation at this conference, their labor requirements go beyond the needs of the construction phase of installing infrastructure. Jobs in plant management, operation and maintenance, as well as personal and professional positions in the service sector, require labor forces at various levels of training beyond the availability of manpower and training capacity for the foreseeable future. Thus, the oil exporting countries have needed and will continue to need to import labor unless they radically alter development plans.

Labor importers have adopted a policy of temporary labor, either geared to a specific project or based on the principle of rotation. The receiving countries do not define themselves as immigration countries, on the model of the U.S. or Canada. Rather they have followed the model of European guestworker countries, which pursued a policy of permitting temporary labor to help in the expansion of postwar economies. Like the industrial nations of Europe, Arab labor importers are currently questioning labor imports and the rotation policy, primarily on social and political grounds. It is well to remember that European questioning of the guestworker policy first started in the late 1960s on the grounds of "over-foreignization." After the 1973 oil boycott, the increase in energy prices, and the recession, economic questions (such as unemployment and job competition) came to the forefront. It is clear, even in the European case, that foreign workers are not always redundant and easily disposable. In Europe, they were structurally integrated into the industrial base in areas like auto manufacturing, as well as in the operation of infrastructure like local transportation. Birks, in his presentation, makes a similar point with regard to the oil exporters in the Middle East. Although social and political costs are currently a major worry regarding labor imports, the economies being developed will require continued use of foreign labor. The need for foreign labor is not temporary (at least not for the foreseeable future) but a structural necessity, given domestic labor force supplies and training profiles and the type of development being pursued.

Within this context, Middle Eastern labor importers are pursuing a labor rotation policy. A number of policy goals are being pursued simultaneously which require judicious and delicate balancing. These include: meeting labor requirements for projects; balancing Arabic and Pan-Islamic goals; trying to insure that workers leave; diversifying sources of labor so as not to become overly dependent on regional sources; manpower development of the domestic labor force; and maintaining the cultural, economic, and political hegemony of the indigenous populations and ruling elites.

Arab foreign workers present the biggest problem to labor importers for they are the most likely to settle, to be joined by family, and, perhaps, ultimately to make economic, social, and political demands. This is a further reason (in addition to concerns about costs in wages and social overhead and availability) that East and South Asian labor sources are increasingly utilized and will continue to be used, as Birks has pointed out. The Korean construction model is seen as an ideal. Not only are the Korean firms very competitive in terms of price, quality, and timeliness, but the companies also take responsibility for the behavior and exit of their workers. Asians from the Indian subcontinent also present advantages since it is assumed that, by and large, they will not settle, will not bring in families, will accept lower wages, and, in the case of Pakistan and Bangladesh, will help further Islamic solidarity. (The last advantage cuts both ways, however. Islamic sending countries may push for preferential access and, perhaps, treatment of their nationals.)

These presumed advantages, however, are short-lived and certainly would not permit a policy of going outside the region for labor to the virtual exclusion of Arab manpower. The advantages are short-lived because they are limited to a vision of a development stage requiring construction of infrastructure, of discrete projects requiring temporary labor which can then be dispensed with. As in the European case, it is a vision of labor needed for expansion that can be reexported. However, as Birks has shown with his analysis of labor requirements and domestic supplies, this vision is too narrow. Already foreign workers fill jobs slots in the management and operation of the various economies, including the entire range of skill levels from professionals and managers to operatives in transportation.

Neither will the pursuit of a policy of development based on "industrial plantations," operated to a large extent by foreign labor isolated in colonies at the industrial sites, necessarily solve the problem of preventing settlement. In addition, it will be costly and inefficient due to training and rotation of workers. For skilled occupations and managerial and professional level workers involved in high technology plants, and even in the case of the semiskilled, labor rotation may not be compatible with staying competitive. Rotation of workers is not like replacing an oil-filter in an engine.

Even beyond the issue of rotation, there is a question of worker motivation and productivity when the worker is isolated geographically, socially, and politically. Wages become almost the sole incentive. It is not altogther clear that worker morale and productivity will not suffer.

In addition to questioning whether an industrial plantation strategy can produce competitive industries, it should also be pointed out that the approach overlooks the need for foreign workers to man other parts of the economy. Foreign workers cannot be totally isolated physically. They will be needed in areas outside industrial sites. Social and political tensions seem inevitable, given the current course of development in the oil-exporting countries. The construction model and the rotation approach will not completely eliminate the problem of demands from foreign workers, nor will they prevent settlement. Even in 1975, there was about one foreign resident nonworker for each foreign worker in the labor-receiving countries of the Middle East. As requirements change to a need for more highly skilled workers (in sectors other than construction, where the workers' camp facilitates isolation and repatriation), the pressure to allow the residence of family units is likely to increase.

## International Migration of Labor and Stability in the Middle East—1980–1985

This review has emphasized the potential negative impacts of labor migration on sending and receiving countries. On the one hand, the focus has been on issues which are currently being raised in sending countries for which no ready solutions are available. On the other hand, the shortcomings of the policy and approach of labor-importing countries have been emphasized, as they try to balance a number of goals, most importantly access to the labor needed to meet current development targets, with avoidance of settlement and its consequent threat to cultural and political hegemony. How destabilizing is migration of labor likely to be between now and 1985 for sending and receiving countries?

Unless there is a major change in the development plans of oil-exporting countries, Arab labor exporters will probably continue to find a market for their manpower. Insofar as manpower export increases dependency and slows down development in these countries, the value of remittances to the sending countries must be discounted. A large scale net flow of labor back to sending countries and a consequent sharp decline in remittances does not seem probable in the next five years due to voluntary abandonment of current development plans in oil-exporting countries. Arab sending countries, however, cannot assume an ever-expanding flow of remittances. The data from Ecevit (1979) in Table 25 shows the great increases in remittances in the 1970s for a number of labor suppliers to the Middle East. The data on remittances as a percentage of exports and imports not only underscores the appeal of remittances but equally emphasizes dependency. The Algerian and Turkish data also indicate what can happen when outlets for labor contract (in Europe in those cases).

In sum, current advantages, especially from remittances, should not obscure the dependence on remittances, the problems which may result if they fall off, and the manpower shortages that may (and in most cases apparently do) underwrite the remittance flow. The key is labor demand, a factor beyond the control of labor exporters. Should demand rapidly decline, the Turkish case provides some experience on likely economic and political impacts.

Receiving countries, despite their fears about the social and political potential of a large foreign workforce and foreign resident population, do not seem to be altering the direction of development strategy. It seems unlikely that the foreign population will be a major destabilizing factor in the near future, but, clearly, the large foreign population could exacerbate economic or political problems should they arise. There are no signs of any growing movement by foreign workers which would question or threaten stability. On the contrary, the current policy on and the position of foreigners can arguably be seen as reinforcing the social and economic structures of the receiving countries (and even of the sending countries). Some would even argue that a new kind of development, dependent on foreign labor, kept in a politically and socially inferior position, may be taking place. Modern versions of the Athenian city-state, composed of citizens and metics, may be emerging. Whatever the ultimate instability of such arrangements, it is not immediately obvious that such a situation

# Table 25

Flow of Workers' Remittances Expressed as a Percentage of Total Imports and Exports of Goods in Selected Labor-Exporting Countries

| Country | 1974 | | | 1975 | | | 1976 | | | 1977 | | |
|---|---|---|---|---|---|---|---|---|---|---|---|---|
| | Remit-tances[1] | As % of Exports | As % of Imports | Remit-tances | As % of Exports | As % of Imports | Remit-tances | As % of Exports | As % of Imports | Remit-tances | As % of Exports | As % of Imports |
| Algeria | 390 | 9 | 9 | 466 | 11 | 7 | 245 | 5 | 4 | 246 | 4 | 3 |
| Bangladesh | 35 | 10 | 2 | 35 | 9 | 1 | 36 | 10 | 1 | 83 | 18 | 9 |
| Egypt | 189 | 11 | 5 | 367 | 23 | 7 | 754 | 47 | 18 | 1,425 | 66 | 27 |
| India | 276 | 8 | 5 | 490 | 12 | 8 | 750[2] | 17 | 12 | | | 20 |
| Jordan | 75 | 48 | 12 | 167 | 109 | 18 | 396 | 198 | 34 | 425 | 186 | 38 |
| Morocco | 356 | 21 | 17 | 533 | 35 | 18 | 548 | 43 | 16 | 577 | 44 | 18 |
| Pakistan | 151 | 15 | 6 | 230 | 22 | 8 | 353 | 31 | 12 | 1,118 | 88 | 40 |
| Syrian Arab Republic | 62 | 8 | 4 | 55 | 6 | 3 | 51[2] | 5 | 2 | | | 7 |
| Tunisia | 118 | 13 | 9 | 146 | 17 | 8 | 135 | 17 | 8 | 142 | 16 | 8 |
| Turkey | 1,425 | 93 | 33 | 1,312 | 94 | 25 | 982 | 50 | 17 | 982 | 56 | 17 |
| Yemen Arab Republic | 159 | 1,325 | 69 | 221 | 1,556 | 72 | 525 | 4,269 | 137 | 1,013 | 5,449 | 139 |
| Yemen P.D.K. | 41 | 410 | 23 | 56 | 373 | 32 | 115 | 261 | 40 | 179 | 352 | 49 |

[1] In current prices, million dollars, gross figures.
[2] Estimates.

Source: Ecevit, Zafer H. "International Labor Migration in the Middle East and North Africa: Trends, Effects and Policies." Paper presented to the Rockefeller Foundation Conference on International Migration, Bellagio, Italy; June, 1979.

may not last for some time. Allowing for arguments on both sides of that issue, it does not seem likely that, *within five years*, foreign resident populations will challenge the economic and political systems that provide material advantages to imported labor.

It is clear that international migration of labor involves contradictions and tensions for sending and receiving countries. That these contradictions and tensions are manageable in the short term, especially given the individual and societal advantages that result from labor flows, has been demonstrated in the Middle East, in Europe, in North America, in Southern Africa and elsewhere. Labor migration and the presence of foreign populations seem unlikely to trigger instability in the Middle East in the next five years. However, they can fuel the flames if instability arises from other sources in the near future, and, therefore, the horizon of twenty years hence is another question.

# Part III:
# Other Determinants: Corporate,
# Congressional, Military

# Rebuilding America's Productive Capacity: The Potential for Business and Economic Development in the Middle East

## BY JOHN V. JAMES

AMERICA HAS ALWAYS been at her best in crisis situations—when we, her people, have had our backs to the wall, when we have been at the crossroads so to speak. That's when we always have taken a hard, objective look at ourselves, fully examined the strategic options available to us, and then aggressively pursued proper courses of affirmative action. That's what we did to win our independence more than 200 years ago. That's what we did to work our way out of the Great Depression. That's what we did to stop the Third Reich. And that's exactly what we must do now to meet the most pressing challenge of contemporary America—the challenge of reindustrialization.

*Reindustrialization* has truly become a buzz word in our great country, a term whose meaning has manifested itself as a result of the critical need for America to enhance her competitive strength at home and abroad. Everywhere we turn, the national media and other molders of public opinion are focusing long-overdue attention on our economic dilemma and its potentially dire implications, including the very real possibility of a shrinking standard of living for most of our citizens in this decade of the eighties and beyond. Americans at all levels of the social and economic spectrum are confronted with the prospect of a national lifestyle that reflects diminishing real disposable income and less discretionary purchasing power for the nonessentials that so often enhance the quality of the human experience. After a decade of increases in take-home pay somewhat obscuring or mitigating the escalating cost of living, we have awakened—and none too soon—to find that the American dream is becoming a nightmare of eroding economic security.

A look at these statistics shows why: we had a standard of living that

153

ranked only fifth in the world last year, after having been first as recently as 1972; we had inflation that for the first time in history was higher than the average of all industrial nations in 1979; we had a 23 percent decline in our share of world markets during the decade of the seventies. The list goes on and on, and the sobering message it conveys is loud and clear. It tells us we must move swiftly and decisively to modernize and expand the nation's industrial base or the personal opportunities that have made America the envy of the free world could fall victim to our own inaction.

If my reading of the country is accurate, rank and file citizens not only are heeding the message but appear to be in no mood for overly simplistic, politically expedient responses to it. There seems, for example, to be a growing awareness that we must eliminate government regulations that impede rather than expand the productive capacity of American industry or we will strongly increase the likelihood of chronic stagflation—the worst of both economic worlds—runaway inflation coupled with stifling recession. There seems to be a growing awareness that we can only accelerate economic growth if we adopt personal and business tax incentives that will revitalize the lagging investment climate in this country and thereby generate the massive amounts of capital it will take to bring forth the new and advanced technologies needed to increase productivity and reduce cost-price pressures. There seems to be a growing awareness that, in addition to rethinking tax policies, government should also support efforts to improve the nation's balance of trade position over the long term. Otherwise, the drain of funds leaving this country to pay for imported oil will not only limit capital formation domestically but will continue to undermine confidence in the dollar. There seems to be an emerging consensus that we must enhance our competitiveness abroad to offset the drain of funds and also because we have lost an important part of the nonenergy domestic market to foreign competitors that will be hard to regain.

Viewed from that perspective, it is unlikely that the necessity or the support for the U.S. aggressively to pursue world trade has ever been greater than now. And I submit that no region offers more opportunity for doing this than the Middle East. It is truly the right place at the right time for America, a region where the demand for a vast array of technology, products, services, and managerial expertise is matched only by the purchasers' ability to pay. The Middle East, including the Arab League states of North Africa, is literally awash in cash. Our imports from there, mainly oil, totaled more than $25 billion in 1979. Services and joint ventures added billions more.

The resulting accumulation of revenues is not only being invested in the capital markets of the U.S. and Europe but is also being plowed into Middle East and Third World economic and business development. The Bank of England reported last summer that Saudi Arabia, Kuwait, the United Arab Emirates, and Qatar had $36 billion in cash surplus available in 1979, up from $6 billion in 1973. A report by First National of Chicago indicates that Saudi Arabia's current surplus could be $41 billion for 1980 and $32 billion for 1981. Iraq, OPEC's second largest oil producer, has a surplus of roughly $20 billion that has been growing fast, according to reliable sources. Barring an unforeseen disaster, the war with Iran has imposed only a temporary restraint on the rate of surplus growth.

Last year, the first ten countries in the Middle East in terms of purchases from the U.S. were, in descending order: Saudi Arabia, $4.9 billion; Israel, $1.9 billion; Egypt, $1.4 billion; Iran, $1 billion; Kuwait, $765 million; The United Arab Emirates, $667 million; Libya, $468 million; Iraq, $442 million; Algeria, $404 million; and Turkey, $354 million. While the Middle East total of $14.3 billion is up substantially from a decade ago, the fact remains that our trade in the region is just a little more than half of what we are importing from there, and we probably account for less than 20 percent of the region's overall imports. Therefore, the margin for further U.S. penetration is clearly sizable.

Moreover, as OPEC acknowledged in a report during the summer, the major oil-producing countries, including those located in the Middle East, should look increasingly to the industrialized world for help in realizing their growth objectives. Specifically, OPEC said that in negotiating with the U.S. and other developed nations concerning oil purchases, its members should seek from them access to technology and greater involvement in exploration activities through both investment and provision of expertise in joint research and training. OPEC also urged its members to try to obtain aid for their downstream petroleum industries by inducing developed nations to have trade barriers and other restrictions that hinder the movement of petrochemical production from developing countries removed. In return, OPEC said its members should be willing to offer, and I quote, "A certain degree of assurance on security of oil supply."

The bottom line is this: they need us, and we obviously need them, not only for their oil but as immense, potentially lucrative markets that could serve as a foundation for the vigorous expansion of international commerce. We must initiate that expansion to rectify our debilitating balance of trade deficit and the many problems attendant to it.

In Saudi Arabia, downstream petroleum activities do not currently extend to petrochemicals, but the Kingdom is launching a multibillion-dollar entry into that market sector. Furthermore, plans to offer attractive incentive oil supplies to joint venture companies have made participation all the more appealing to them and the suppliers of the broad range of equipment and materials utilized in building and maintaining petrochemical plants. The Saudis have emphasized infrastructure development in recent years—putting into place the roads, harbors, airports, housing, schools, telecommunications, and the like needed to support downstream operations that would compete in the world marketplace against American interests.

But, if any American supplier is reluctant to become involved with their downstream operations because they would compete someday with U.S. companies, let him be assured that such misguided loyalty would be as naïve as it is counterproductive. Most executives would tell you that this would constitute a classic example of cutting off your nose to spite your face, because the Arab world is not dependent on American suppliers. If we do not support Arab expansion efforts, you can rest assured that somebody will from Japan, West Germany, France, Italy, or Great Britain. The Arabs have these alternatives, and more.

Virtually all American products and services face intense competition in the Middle East and other world markets—the technical superiority we enjoyed in the immediate post-World War II period no longer exists. All reasonably well-developed countries have joined us in possessing the ability to generate highly sophisticated technology. With a few exceptions, their capabilities are comparable to ours across the board. Thus, today's nationalism can only serve to limit tomorrow's growth potential. Put another way, we cannot let ill-advised protectionist arguments stand in the way of a much-needed growth philosophy. We are entering a period of history in which industry will be required to stand on its own two feet—to succeed or fail as performance dictates. Performance will be determined by the quality of our technology, the quality of our management, and the quality of our workmanship. These basic factors in turn require a certain quality of will or attitude—precisely the attitude I am setting forth now.

Among the twenty-five nations of the Middle East and Arab world, Saudi Arabia is not alone in stepping up downstream petroleum activity. Iraq, Libya, Qatar, and the United Arab Emirates are among others with active programs. In addition, Turkey is pushing for increased foreign participation in its oil-exploration efforts, encouraging joint ventures and setting up a state fund within its central bank to finance activity with long-term, low-interest loans.

Egypt is another major market that will offer American business many favorable trade and investment opportunities during the 1980s. As I noted earlier, U.S. exports to Egypt were $1.4 billion last year, or 22 percent of its total market, and future prospects are excellent for equipment in such fields as electrical power generation and distribution, computers, communications, construction and mining, and agriculture. Sales of consumer durables are expected to remain good also. Egypt has an "open door" policy to generate foreign participation in joint ventures, and there are tax incentives and other inducements that should appeal to prospective participants. Priority is currently being given to industries that produce cement, iron bars, sheet glass, clay, bricks, and a variety of consumer goods. On some large capital projects in Egypt involving the U.S. Agency for International Development, procurement is limited to U.S. sources.

Another location with numerous growth opportunities in the Middle East is the United Arab Emirates, which pumps nearly 1.5 million barrels of oil per day. Planned development there includes giant LNG and LPG complexes and a fertilizer plant, and a major industrial diversification program is underway in which foreign investment is encouraged on a participation basis. In seeking to broaden the base of the country's income away from oil, the UAE is establishing a giant industrial complex at Jebel Ali, with the necessary infrastructure facilities to support a wide range of industries. The UAE also plans to join forces with Saudi Arabia and Iraq to set up a $3 billion arms industry, and Iraq reportedly is allocating close to a billion dollars for establishment of an electronics industry by French companies to produce consumer products as well as radar for coastal defense, warships, and warplanes.

While the Sudan is not an oil-exporting nation, it possesses a wealth of natural resources that remains untapped, and, like many other lesser-developed countries in the region, it is exploring positive ways to attract exporters and private investment in the decade of the 1980s and beyond.

One of the region's smaller countries, Bahrain, is located in the Arabian Gulf and not only provides some business opportunities but is booming as a banking center. It hosts fifty-two offshore banking units, which are foreign branches of major banks around the world, and they do not have to maintain monetary reserves with the Bahrain monetary agency. This means that they can be very competitive by charging lower interest rates, particularly in large-scale transactions.

Obviously, I cannot do justice here to the myriad opportunities the Middle East region affords American business. Thus I have touched only on some in a few of the countries to give those unfamiliar with the area a feel for what is available. The examples I used should not be construed in any way as an endorsement of them versus others in the region that may well be equally or more attractive to U.S. companies. What should be clear from even these few illustrations is the great variety of opportunities in all fields of business that the Middle East affords the American business community—not just for the giants among us, but also for those enterprising medium and small concerns.

Those who don't have established organizations in the Middle East can obtain specific leads and other pertinent information about opportunities there by contacting the U.S. Department of Commerce, the U.S.-Arab Chamber of Commerce, or embassies and consulates that the various countries have in Washington. The Middle East Research Institute can also provide valuable information services. I cannot stress enough that the opportunities are there; it's just a matter of exploring and capitalizing on them. Yet, how well we do that—how well we actually compete in the Middle East and elsewhere—will depend, as I noted at the outset of my remarks, on our will to do so, both as a nation and as individuals.

The late Bishop Brooke Foss Wescott of Cambridge once said, "Silently and imperceptibly, as we wake or sleep, we grow strong or weak, and at last some crisis shows what we have become." Let us hope our response to the crisis of reindustrialization will show that we have retained a strong enough measure of the American legacy of determination and resourcefulness. I pray that our "can do" fervor has not mellowed, but, in all candor, I do see signs of weakness in that regard that must be toned up—and fast. It seems at times that we have become immobilized. We seem to be tentative, reluctant, these days. We seem to have a fear of failure when it comes to international business involvement, and to a lot of other challenges for that matter. In the vernacular of football, we seem to be in a prevent defense, protecting a lead that no longer exists, playing for a tie or just to keep it close. We seem, in a word, to lack the assertiveness we once had, and I think I know why.

Maybe we have come eye-ball to eye-ball with government disincentives once too often and finally blinked. Maybe the erosion of our longtime position of strength in world markets has occurred because of governmental policies that have served to inhibit our responsiveness to global needs. Maybe the reliability of America as a source of supply is being questioned—and for good reason—because of the manner in which the U.S. government has inconsistently formulated and implemented international trade policies, vacillating back and forth with the political tides, thereby causing often bitter animosities to develop between our country and its highly industrialized trading allies, our country and communist powers, and our country and third world nations. Maybe our trading partners see as deterrents to business involvement our foreign corrupt practices act, which severely limits corporate payments or fees to obtain contracts abroad or our corporate tax law, which forces U.S. companies to pay taxes on distributions of foreign subsidiary earnings, even though they also may have met foreign tax requirements on them, or our individual tax laws, which determine eligibility by citizenship rather than residence and add to the personnel cost of U.S. firms operating abroad. Maybe they also feel that way about our trade embargoes, which limit sales of grain and high-technology equipment, our human rights policy, which limits trade with certain countries that violate our codes related to personal freedom, our antitrust laws, which prohibit U.S. corporations from establishing joint trading companies, our export-import bank restrictions, which limit the subsidized credit the U.S. can provide for financing exports, and our health, safety, and environmental regulations, which enforce strict standards for overseas operations of U.S. companies.

Maybe, just maybe, those are among the principal disincentives that cost the U.S. at least $5 billion to $10 billion annually in exports. That is an estimate in *Business Week* received from a leading Commerce Department official, who admitted the actual amount could be closer to $100 billion, and it does not even include joint ventures and services. MERI economists have calculated that every billion dollars in trade American business generates in the Middle East, or elsewhere abroad, maintains at least 30,000—and by some reckonings as many as 50,000—jobs in this country. Moreover, of fundamental importance is the fact that the national interest is served in direct proportion to the degree of success enjoyed by American private enterprise in overseas markets such as the Middle East. The influence our government possesses in the region is reinforced and extended by the private sector's ability to trade and provide technical assistance. These surely ought to be powerful arguments for persuading authorities in Washington not to act in ways that handicap American business in competing for any foreign market.

As counterproductive as they can be, however, governmental disincentives are not the sole source of our nation's competitive decline. Few are more vocal in their criticism of government policies than I, but we in the private sector also are responsible in part for the sagging American economy. Maybe our problems also stem from the fact that when the going gets tough some industries in recent years have been too reliant on the government to cushion the impact for them. We all know that happens far too often, but we are aware, too, of situations in which foreign governments are, in fact, creating unfair advantages for their companies and, therefore, drawing very legitimate complaints from our domestic industries. Thus, in addition to modifying counterproductive positions that hamper our competitive posture, the U.S. must use its influence to stop anticompetitive practices of foreign governments, or consider allowing us to operate under the same ground rules.

Some companies in the U.S. also restrict their own ability to compete abroad by failing to familiarize themselves with the very real cultural differences and market conditions which exist there. According to Abdullah T. Dabbagh, commercial counselor at the Saudi Embassy in Washington, a big part of the competitive problem in the Middle East arises from misconceptions held by U.S. business:

*Misconception number 1*: Doing business in the Arab world is just like doing business anywhere else—the same methods apply.

*Misconception number 2*: The Arab markets are so mysterious, and the people, the prohibitions, and the customs are so different that it is nearly impossible to make a sale.

*Misconception number 3*: The Arabs have so much money that just having the right connections is all that counts; price doesn't really make much difference.

*Misconception number 4*: Arabs in general and Saudi Arabians in particular are very nitpicking; but don't worry, they can't get American quality anywhere else, so they will come around.

Attitudes are really at the crux of the problem, Mr. Dabbagh said, and American businessmen must reshape theirs if they are to tap further the Middle East market.

Businessmen were not the only ones to draw criticism from Mr. Dabbagh. He pointed out that the government's ABSCAM scheme was deeply resented by the Saudis. What ABSCAM seemed to be saying, he believes, is that Arabs are easy to trick, have more money than they know what to do with, and normally do business by fixing officials with money under the table. ABSCAM has promoted the process of stereotyping the Arab as a sinister character in the U.S. He charged that the media of this country have been portraying Arabs negatively: "If we invest in this country," he said, "we are trying to buy it. If we don't invest, we are not recycling our surplus dollars, and we are trying to hurt the American economy." What Mr. Dabbagh is getting at is that we must eliminate misconceptions by truly orienting ourselves to the Middle East marketplace, just as extensively, I might add, as we do in our American markets. We must get away from the type of thinking that prompted Edward R. Murrow to say that "People think they are thinking when they are really just rearranging their prejudices."

Another way U.S. companies fail to realize their potential in the Middle East and other key international markets is by being too inflexible: we sometimes do not exhibit the adaptability it takes to succeed there. A recent report by the Committee for Economic Development noted that if the U.S. is to advance its goals of further penetration of world markets, manufacturing products more efficiently, and exploring the vast reservoir of materials located throughout the world, its multinational companies must demonstrate a greater willingness to live with the restraints imposed on them by host governments, local businesses, and international political and economic conditions.

We must, for example, keep an open mind on working arrangements and approaches such as the sharing of technology and joint ventures. The oil-producing nations of the Middle East simply are not going to deplete further their valuable resources without a commensurate commitment on our part to technology transfer and equity participation. Joint ventures offer genuine advantages in many Middle East countries. In Saudi Arabia, for instance, you reap all the benefits allotted to national industries, including corporate tax exemption for ten years, exemption from duties on materials and machinery, land in industrial estates, and preferential treatment for government purchases.

If we are truly serious about expanding our involvement in Saudi Arabia, Mr. Dabbagh advises—and I can confirm from our experiences at Dresser—that you also will need a sponsor, agent, or representative. Otherwise, the barriers of language, knowledge of market conditions, and the like will handicap you.

We must also overcome past reluctance to trade with socialist countries. While the major socialist countries of the Middle East do not generally allow equity investment by foreign firms, they usually offer rather attractive inducements involving cost-plus deals and generous service contracts.

Additionally, we must exhibit greater willingness to provide assistance in marketing foreign-produced products throughout the world. More American companies need to offer their training expertise in host countries, perhaps even to individuals who do not work for them if the government feels that would be beneficial to the overall business climate there. That's flexibility, and it represents the sort of enlightened thinking American-based companies must adopt if they are to excel in the Middle East.

Finally, American companies tend to travel the safe, tried-and-true path too often. We have become increasingly risk conscious of late. As former Secretary of State James F. Byrnes once commented, "Too many people are thinking of security instead of opportunity. They seem to be more afraid of life than death." The nothing ventured, nothing gained mentality must be revived in this country, because playing it safe is still another of the reasons we have been losing our competitive edge here as well as abroad.

Please don't misconstrue what I am saying. There is nothing inherently unsavory about security, but it should be a byproduct of a successful business endeavor, not the motivating force behind it. International business can be not only good economics, as is its purpose, but can also provide a vital form of security by further strengthening strategic regions of the world such as the Middle East where a weakened posture could serve to threaten the precarious balance of power between East and West. For those nations where unrest and upheaval are more likely, political risk coverage is readily available through the overseas private investment corporation or private insurers to help mitigate the impact of such actions as expropriation, destruction, or cancellation of export and import licenses. Of course, there is no way to eliminate or protect against risk totally: our future will nearly always be fraught with hazards, even failure. We must acknowledge that and exert a greater boldness in pressing onward to maintain our accustomed position in the very forefront of human progress.

I think we would all concur that the state of economic affairs in this country is at a pivotal juncture. In very real jeopardy, if we continue along the road of sagging industrial proficiency, are both the quantity and quality of our lives. Yet there is no question in my mind that if we apply ourselves in meeting the challenge of reindustrialization the way we always have in the face of past national adversities, if we channel the dynamic human attributes of tenacity and ingenuity toward realizing our vast potential in the Middle East and other world markets, we can revitalize our economy and generate the level of profitable growth needed in the years ahead.

If we in business, labor, and academia can mobilize ourselves and our government into an effective constituency dedicated to unleashing the private-enterprise system for a higher degree of global business development, we not only will achieve that end, but we will also gain the residual benefit of long-term peace and understanding among nations that can be derived from it. Let us return to our respective communities personally committed to the establishment of such a constituency and to the formulation of sound, appropriate strategies for assuring the kind of future we all want for ourselves and succeeding generations.

# Outlook for Congressional Actions Affecting Middle East Business

## By Raymond Garcia

SEVERAL MONTHS AGO the American Businessmen's Group of Riyadh, Saudi Arabia, declared in a position paper on "America's Loss of Business in the Middle East" that: "U.S. companies operating in the Middle East are at a competitive disadvantage with European and Asian firms because of U.S. legislation and executive action which restricts and is often punitive as compared to governmental support by other nations for their companies overseas." The group called on the United States Congress to "recognize this situation and to enact immediate legislation which would: "eliminate taxes on American expatriates which force U.S. firms to hire foreigners or price themselves out of the market; provide financing for American firms which would put them on a competitive footing with foreign firms; and rationalize antitrust, antiboycott, anticorruption and other laws which penalize U.S. firms abroad without advancing any significant policy objectives."

Today, I should like to discuss the status of and the outlook for congressional action on four of the principal export impediments cited in the American Businessmen's position paper: (1) Taxation of Americans overseas; (2) the Foreign Corrupt Practices Act; (3) U.S. antiboycott legislation; and (4) export financing.

At no time since President Eisenhower announced the beginning of the National Export Expansion Program in March 1960 has the Congress been so committed to action to promote U.S. export growth. Both in the House and the Senate, legislators have organized themselves in export caucuses. Bills have been introduced to lift or lighten many of the regulatory burdens on exporting. President Carter sent to the Congress messages identifying and analyzing export disincentives and had proposed, before his election defeat, to make some progress in their removal. But this session of Congress will end without any action having been taken, and we must await a new Congress and a new president to determine whether the momentum to improve our international trade posture will continue. What is the likelihood that this will happen? Let us look at each of the four issues I have mentioned.

## The Taxation of Americans Abroad

Nearly sixty years ago, Congress exempted Americans working overseas from being taxed on their overseas income. Congress wanted to encourage foreign trade, because it recognized that U.S. exports depended to some extent on the presence of Americans overseas, who would buy goods from home to serve their needs abroad.

The tax treatment of overseas income was revised in the 1950s to end the abuses of highly paid movie stars. Congress imposed a $20,000 limit on the foreign-earned income that could be excluded from tax and altered the foreign-residency requirements. Further revisions were made in the 1960s limiting the amounts of income excluded. For up to three years abroad, $20,000 could be excluded; income greater than these amounts was taxed, beginning at the lowest marginal rates, and foreign taxes on the excluded income could be credited against any U.S. taxes owed.

By 1976, Congress no longer was convinced of the value of lenient tax treatment for Americans working abroad. The Tax Reform Act of 1976 reduced the exclusion to $15,000 (except for workers in charitable organizations) and repealed the bracket adjustment. These revisions, together with certain tax-court decisions, could have had the unintended consequence for some Americans of making them liable for taxes amounting to more than the income they had earned. As soon as Congress realized its mistake, it retroactively repealed the law.

It was superseded by the Foreign Earned Income Act of 1978. This replaced the earned income exclusion with a set of deductions to offset the higher cost of living, housing and education abroad, and the transportation costs of annual home leave. Americans working in certain "hardship" areas, principally in the Middle East, were allowed an additional $5,000 deduction, and hardship area workers residing in camps could elect a $20,000 exclusion instead of the deductions.

However, these revisions have proven inadequate as well. American companies have had to pay higher salaries to compensate for the additional tax burden that resulted from repeal of the exclusion and higher salary demands have forced American companies to reduce the number of U.S. citizens working abroad and to hire more foreign nationals. Thus, the U.S. presence overseas has declined, negatively impacting the demand for U.S. exports. These were the findings of a study on the "Economic Impact of Changing Taxation of U.S. Workers Overseas," prepared by Chase Econometric Associates, Inc. for the U.S. and Overseas Tax Fairness Committee in June 1980.

Such arguments and others have persuaded members of Congress and President Carter to propose alternative forms of tax relief. The Economic Revitalization Plan that President Carter announced on August 28 provided for an exclusion on all earnings up to $25,000 plus 10 percent of the next $60,000 earned abroad, but they could be targeted only to those working in "hardship" areas. Also in August, the Senate Finance Committee approved an elective exclusion of $50,000 ($65,000 after two years abroad) plus an excess housing costs deduction, but only for those workers in developing countries or those whose jobs were export-related. However, neither these nor other proposals seem likely to be enacted this year.

Because a new Congress begins in 1981, all pending legislation will have to be reintroduced to be considered. With the substantial support that reform of the tax provisions for overseas Americans has enjoyed in the 96th Congress, it is highly probable that similar legislation will be considered in the 97th Congress. Moreover, given President Reagan's commitment to improving U.S. economic activity both at home and abroad and the fact that key members of Mr. Reagan's transition advisory team are quite familiar with these tax problems, there is a strong likelihood that the Reagan administration will also lend its support to this reform. The provisions governing overseas Americans probably will be included in the tax cut legislation that President Reagan will send to the Congress and so could be among the first pieces of legislation that Congress will consider next year. Thus, the question is not *whether* there will be tax relief for Americans working abroad, but *how much* it will be and *how soon* it will come. The most likely outcome is that sometime in 1981, the Congress will approve, and the president will sign, a bill containing a two-tiered exclusion, possibly $25,000 in general and $50,000 for those in hardship areas, and that this relief will be made retroactive to January 1, 1981.

## Foreign Corrupt Practices Act

In December 1977 the Foreign Corrupt Practices Act became law. It declared illegal the bribery by U.S. firms of foreign officials or political candidates to obtain or retain business abroad and mandated the keeping of accurate books to assure detection of wrongdoing. Severe penalties were provided for violations; a $1 million fine on a corporation or $10,000 on an individual. Jurisdiction over enforcement was divided between the Securities and Exchange Commission and the Justice Department, with the SEC responsible for civil prosecution of firms having SEC-registered securities and the Justice Department responsible for criminal prosecutions.

Since its enactment, businessmen have complained that the act lacked clarity and that this impeded overseas business for fear of incrimination. For example, businessmen want to know to what extent they are responsible for having "reason to know" that a foreign agent is not using part of his commission as a bribe to a foreign official. What is the definition of a foreign official? What is permissible entertainment and gift-giving? Do local laws and customs have precedence over U.S. laws? These and many other questions have been asked about the law and guidance has been sought to eliminate the ambiguities.

In September 1978, President Carter announced that he had asked the Justice Department to give the business community guidance concerning its "enforcement" priorities under the act. This the Justice Department has done, and, in March of this year, it also announced a review procedure. Under this procedure, companies concerned about the possibility of violating the act can give Justice the details of the prospective transaction abroad and receive advice as to whether Justice would take enforcement action under the act were the transaction to proceed further.

The procedure, however, has many problems. Senator John Chafee (R-R.I.), in an interview in *International Construction Newsletter*, indicated that the Justice Department is not required to provide an opinion in every case, nor within a definite time period, nor can general policies be inferred from any one opinion. Furthermore, information that companies give the Justice Department is not exempt from disclosure under the Freedom of Information Act and other agencies are not bound by the Justice Department's opinions. However, the SEC recently said that it would temporarily recognize the Justice Department's opinions, but only on a pilot basis until May 1981.

To address these and other problems with the Foreign Corrupt Practices Act (FCPA), Senator Chafee introduced on May 28, 1980, the proposed "Business Accounting and Foreign Trade Simplification Act." No action is expected on the bill this session. Senator Chafee intends to reintroduce the bill, with some changes, in January 1981. Senator Jake Garn (R-Utah), the new chairman of the Senate Committee on Banking, Housing and Urban Affairs, probably will hold hearings on the bill early next session.

A bill similar to Chafee's will probably be introduced in the House by Reps. James Broyhill (R-N.C.) and Matthew Rinaldo (R-N.J.). They are members of the Consumer Protection and Finance Subcommittee of the House Interstate and Foreign Commerce Committee, which originated the FCPA in the House.

With strong business support, there is an excellent chance that the FCPA can be reformed to permit legitimate export sales to be made without fear of needless government interference.

## Antiboycott Legislation

The federal government has three different statutes regulating the responses of American companies to the boycotts by foreign countries of other countries. These statutes are administered by four different government agencies. In addition, twelve states have enacted antiboycott legislation of much broader scope than the federal versions.

The three federal laws are:

(1) Provisions of the tax code (Section 999, referred to as the "Ribicoff Amendment") which deny certain tax benefits to parties agreeing to participate in or cooperate with foreign boycotts. These are administered by the Treasury Department;

(2) Provisions of the Export Administration Act, which expressly prohibit taking or agreeing to take certain types of actions with intent to comply with or support foreign boycotts of other countries. These are administered by the Department of Commerce; and

(3) Provisions of the antitrust laws, which are administered by the Justice Department and the Federal Trade Commission.

The tax provisions and the provisions of the Export Administration Act conflict with each other in several important ways, such as who is subject to the law, who is protected and what activities are exempt. Although the Treasury and Commerce Departments have tried to reduce and harmonize the differences by issuing, where possible, common interpretations, there remain intractable differences that can be altered only by legislation and not by further interpretation.

What is the likelihood that the confusing clashes of three different federal statutes can be rationalized so as to reduce or remove an impediment to U.S. exports? Let us take these provisions in order and see what appears to make the greatest sense.

First, the tax provisions. These were enacted in 1976, in haste in a conference committee of the House Ways and Means Committee and the Senate Finance Committee, without any hearings or prior consideration. They were pushed through because their proponents were fearful that Congress would not pass legislation strictly prohibiting U.S. compliance with foreign boycotts and providing severe penalties for violations. This fear proved unfounded. The Export Administration (EAA) was enacted in 1977, satisfying most interested parties that a reasonably proper balance had been struck between outlawing foreign boycott compliance and permitting legitimate trade to continue. Subsequent enforcement of the EAA has also generally satisfied the various private sector groups that enforcement was evenhanded.

Since the EAA provisions involved extended congressional hearings and consideration, substantial participation by all interested private sector groups, and delicate negotiations and compromises among them, followed by lengthy debates on the floors of both houses of Congress, it is logical to conclude that the tax provisions could be repealed or harmonized with the EAA provisions without compromising the integrity of U.S. antiboycott policies. Given the goodwill of all sides on this issue, it is possible that such a result could be achieved in the 97th Congress as part of the tax cut proposals that inevitably will be proposed early in the session.

Changes in the EAA provisions are less likely to be sought or achieved. Assuming that the act will not be altered before its termination date of September 30, 1983, Congress will probably not consider revisions until 1982. Since the antiboycott provisions represented such a delicate balance of conflicting interests, only the most major deficiencies are likely to be considered and even then changes might not be proposed for fear of unraveling the compromise. Thus, I would be reluctant to cite any possible areas for change without there being some evidence of damage to any interested party. One provision of the EAA which is before the courts is the prohibition on providing factual information on one's own business relationship with others to a boycotting country. The suing parties allege that the provision is an abridgement of the Constitutional guarantees of free speech and right to due process. Should these cases be decided in favor of the plaintiffs, then changes in the statute are likely.

No pressure to change the antitrust provisions is apparent, perhaps because the Justice Department is not expected to use the provisions for antiboycott enforcement again as long as the EAA is effectively enforced.

To summarize, therefore, I see the probability of repeal or revision of the tax provisions in 1981, possibly some consideration of change in the EAA in 1982, to become effective on October 1, 1983, and no change in the antitrust provisions concerning U.S. compliance with foreign boycotts.

## Export Financing

In recent years, the Export-Import Bank has had an increasingly difficult time in getting adequate funding from the Congress. Since 1974, the Eximbank has been part of the unified federal budget and each year must seek authority from the Congress for an approved lending level. Because it is considered simultaneously with foreign assistance appropriations requests, the Bank has fallen victim to all of the controversy surrounding U.S. foreign aid and has been held hostage to resolution of foreign-aid disputes.

Supporters of a viable export lending institution are calling for an urgent reexamination of the budgetary treatment accorded the Bank. They argue that unless this treatment is altered, the Bank will not be able to support U.S. exports to the extent enjoyed by the exporters of competitor nations, thus damaging U.S. export efforts.

Several options are under consideration. One is to remove the Bank entirely from the budget. There are several valid accounting reasons for proposing this:

(1) The Bank uses no taxpayer money nor does it receive an annual appropriation;

(2) Exim's loans are treated like other federal expenditures, but are different because they are repaid with interest; and

(3) Exim has paid back all of the initial capital to the Treasury and has made a profit.

While these arguments are logical from an accounting standpoint, they fly in the face of political reality. At a time when Congress and the administration urgently want to control federal spending, there appears to be no likelihood that a proposal to take the Bank "off-budget" will be favorably received, regardless of the force of the argument.

A second option would be to take the Eximbank authorization completely out of the Foreign Assistance Appropriations Act and move it to another part of the budget—to a part that would be considered by other subcommittees of the Congress. This raises questions about where it should go and which bodies of Congress are most likely to treat the Bank kindly.

Because such questions will take considerable time to sort out, depending on organizational and personality considerations relative to an as-yet-unknown administration and Congress, the most likely option for immediate change is a third option. This would remove the annual Bank authorization request from the Foreign Assistance Appropriations Act and give it a separate appropriations request within the foreign affairs budget, as was done for the International Monetary Fund. This option, or a variant of it, will probably be proposed in 1981.

However, whatever treatment is finally given to the Eximbank's budget, the question of the level of funding that the Bank should be authorized must still be answered. The budget-cutters will be severely tested in 1981. All signs point to an alarming growth in federal spending, which growth the Reagan administration will have to address seriously if it is to make a credible attack on inflation. Whether the Bank is in or out of the budget or in or out of the Foreign Assistance Appropriation will have little impact on that fundamental question. Frankly, I am pessimistic about the likelihood of there being any major improvement in raising the lending ceiling of the Bank in the early 1980s, so as to make this American institution competitive with its foreign counterparts. Exporters, along with many other deserving sectors of the economy, will have to share in the burden of sacrifice necessary to put the economy of the United States in order. Perhaps more productive efforts might be directed at persuading competitor nations to exercise a measure of restraint in subsidizing their exports.

In sum, then, I see a possibility for real progress in easing the taxes on Americans working abroad, probably coming in 1981. There is also a good likelihood that some of the burden of the Foreign Corrupt Practices Act will be lifted in 1981 or 1982. Less likely, but still a distinct possibility, assuming the goodwill of all interested parties, is the repeal or harmonization of the antiboycott provisions of the EAA. Least likely is substantial progress in increasing the lending capacity of the Eximbank. All in all, I believe that the outlook for Congressional action to remove some of the significant impediments to U.S. business with the Middle East is very encouraging for the period 1981–1985.

# Military Factors Determining Middle East Security in the Eighties

## By James Noyes

WITH SO MANY STATES in the Middle East ruled by their respective militaries with such enormous investments in arms and training, and with numerous conflicts either ongoing or incipient, any projection for the region to 1985 must weigh the military factors. However, because they are inextricable from social, economic, and political determinants, they are both causes and effects. One may almost ask whether there can be a regional epidemic of political failures that have provoked resort to military force. Morocco battles the Libyan and Algerian-supported Polisario. Libya plays chicken with U.S. reconnaissance aircraft and assembles a huge cache of modern Soviet weapons, while serving as a staging point for Soviet adventures in Africa as well as pursuing its own goals in the area. In Lebanon, private armies of many kinds mix with 30,000 Syrian troops and endure regular Israeli air and sea incursions. In Syria itself, tanks ring many cities in a manner suggesting rule by an army of occupation. The war between Iran and Iraq, the two Yemens which are always on the brink of war, Ethiopia with its thirteen insurgencies—but the list is too long.

On the one hand, these events symbolize political failures but, on the other, the energies released by developments are, in many ways, positive. There is a kind of renaissance of cultural assertiveness which, paradoxically, accompanies the political disintegration. Basic historical factors are evident, but the recent impetus derives from oil wealth, coupled with new levels of military capacity, and is subtly linked to boosted levels of pride following the 1973 Arab-Israeli war and Iran's revolution. There is also a realization that the superpowers in some instances cancel each other out, thereby allowing greater freedom of action for regional states.

In the longer range, the pride and assertiveness that is so evident when coupled with political and cultural reformation will serve as a viable barrier to Soviet designs. Unfortunately, in the meantime, the energies released tend to fragment the states' policies. This process encourages the growth of uncompromising totalitarian or utopian movements. Iran is a good example. Khomeini's brand of transnational radical Islam seeks to unite all Muslims, irrespective of national loyalties. The practical effect, however, virtually destroys the national base from which he preaches. Should this trend spread, the fractures evident in Iran and Lebanon today might be seen in Syria, Iraq, or Pakistan tomorrow.

Although the region's dramatic developments are the product of complex factors, a look at the element of military balances is useful. Acute and highly provocative military imbalances have almost unfailingly provided an opening for major Soviet advances in the area. One can recall the original Soviet arms deals with Egypt and Syria in the mid-fifties and, particularly, the major Soviet surge into Egypt following the 1967 war—as responses to a combination of Western reluctance to provide military support and quantum jumps in Israeli military capability. The situation is similar on the Horn of Africa. Initial Soviet moves into Somalia were in the military supply and training area and were a response to the relative colossus proportions of Ethiopian forces. With the collapse of the Ethiopian empire, Somalia struck militarily into the Ogaden, thereby creating an absolute necessity for Ethiopia to invite Soviets and Cubans to assist in counterinsurgency efforts and in repelling a foreign invader. One could also classify Libya's relationship with the Soviets as one which evolved almost entirely in the military sphere in response to Qadafi's paranoia about Egypt, combined with his burning ambition to play a role on the world stage.

Moving to the present, the course of this reminiscence leads directly to the Iraq-Iran war and to the problems of Pakistan. As Iran's imperial structure collapsed along with most of its military capacity, Iraq could not resist the temptation to attack, particularly as neither superpower seemed likely to respond on behalf of Iran. It was planned as a short war. However, it drags on and the combination of inconclusiveness and erosion of resources appears to create a situation ripe for the Soviets, albeit one carrying acute risks. For neighboring Pakistan, shock waves have come from all sides. After the 1971 breakup of that country, Iran and China gave the surviving portion of Pakistan the semblance of a strategic place in the region. Now, with Iran in shambles and an eclipsed Afghan national identity replaced by a massive Soviet presence, Pakistan's military credibility has all but vanished.

This dreary catalog would be incomplete without mention of the absolute dependence of the Peoples' Democratic Republic of Yemen on Soviet, Cuban and East German military and security support. And, finally, back in the core area of Middle East conflict, there is Syria, whose major political direction over the past few years has been away from the Soviets toward Islamic fundamentalism for some and in search of political democracy for others. Since Camp David and Egypt's adoption of an independent course, Syria's military capability in a relative sense vis-à-vis Israel has been reduced to the level of tokenism. With forces tied down in Lebanon, a collapse of relations with Iraq, and serious problems with Jordan, Syria has become preoccupied with internal security problems precisely at a time of marked vulnerability to external threats. The result, of course, has been the sudden treaty with the Soviet Union and the union with Libya—almost *in extremis* statements of a will to survive, through intervention by Soviet forces if necessary. To the extent that Israeli pressures on Lebanon and hardlining on all negotiating issues have added to pressures on Syria, we have paid a heavy price for our lack of ability to harmonize foreign policy with the Israeli government at a time when their dependence on the U.S. has become so visible.

A review of these military imbalances, while inevitably oversimplified, has utility for a look ahead into the eighties. There are few reasons to assume any reduction in the use of military pressures. In fact, at least in part because the Soviets have generally done so poorly in the region on the political level, it seems fair to assume they are now prepared to become even more aggressive in retaining their footholds in the area through force coupled with the thinnest sort of contrived host invitation as exemplified by the Afghan experience. In short, we should expect to see the Soviets rely increasingly on the strength of their military power as their ability to effect deep ideological penetration in the region, or to equal the West in technological appeal, or as an investment base, declines. While many of the dependencies upon which the Soviets rely are likely to be short term, many, like Ethiopia and the PDRY, probably will span the period of our attention—through 1985. One is likely to be permanent, because it strains the imagination to conjure circumstances in which Soviet forces will fully depart Afghanistan.

How will the U.S. (or the West in general) compare to the Soviets as military supplier and power mentor over the coming years? Except where outclassed in a given situation, such as now pertains to naval forces available in the Arabian Sea, the Soviets have a clear preponderance of nearby power sufficient to exert strong intimidation; they have relatively vast quantities of weapons to sell or to offer during a client's war and they can respond without Congressional debate. While the U.S. retains the advantage of quality of weapons in some areas and usually permits more stockpiling of spares and ammunition, our procedures are cumbersome, our delivery schedules are notoriously slow, and our state of the art technology is so quickly leaked to the media that we generate further multitudinous problems when this frequently still unavailable hardware is "denied" to a foreign purchaser.

All the states in the region have logisticians able to use calculators. The capacities of Soviet airlift have been amply demonstrated. The new Soviet presence in Afghanistan, though a burden politically, adds an obvious new strategic dimension to Soviet power in the Middle East and South Asia. The 24 Soviet ground divisions in the Caucasus, along with 7 airborne divisions and some 500 first-line tactical aircraft, cannot be ignored as a potential factor in any contingency. Similarly, against the leanness of our available supplies and our distance, the Libyan cache of weapons cannot but figure in the political/military regional calculus.

These asymmetries between the U.S. and the Soviets are likely to continue, but, as the U.S. proceeds to correct its overall deficiencies in conventional forces and upgrades its presence in the area, the very existence of the trend itself will reduce one component of Soviet advantage. The greatest U.S. error would lie in trying to imitate the Soviets in acquiring fixed American-staffed and operated bases in Egypt, the Arabian peninsula, or the Horn of Africa. To do so would open the door to the Soviets in an unparalleled fashion (although an exception might be U.S. use of Israeli or Sinai bases, as some have suggested). There are no shortcuts which would provide benefits, in a purely military sense, sufficient to outweigh the disastrous political consequences of such a move, which would also have an adverse military impact on the West. Instead, the U.S. must utilize the political impact of Soviet action in Afghanistan, and the evolutions in Arab alignments stemming from the Iran-Iraq war, to strengthen its political relations with moderate Arab forces. Suppose, for example, the PDRY with Soviet help stages a coup in Oman by 1984 and airlifts sustaining forces from Aden to support a blatantly puppet regime. The chances for a successful blocking action by regional states, undoubtedly assisted by U.S. air and sea forces, will be far greater if the governments of Saudi Arabia and Egypt are relatively strong and have legitimacy in the eyes of their own armed forces. If, on the other hand, the legitimacy of these and other governments of the area has been weakened by a large U.S. military presence, coupled with inadequate U.S. commitment on the core issues of the Arab-Israeli problem, then the presence of even 50,000 American soldiers within a short striking distance will prove of little avail.

The current war in the Persian Gulf, though still obscure as to outcome, provides a convenient focus for many of the politico-military problems of the area. Should a military collapse occur in Iraq or Iran, surely the Soviets will make a major move. Let us assume, however, that both countries will survive more or less intact, that there will be a military stalemate, and that negotiations will take place over a very long period during which each will relapse into limited air, artillery, and guerilla exchanges. What will be the impact of this kind of gradual winding-down on the equations we have just considered? To begin with (although this may appear to be almost trivial), there is no question of the performance of U.S. military equipment and training in yet another Middle East war. No matter what the precise outcome, it appears that the mystique of U.S. quality and general superiority will have been retained despite Iran's ragtag peformance. Iraq, with the advantages of being the attacker, of surprise, and of fully supplied and prepared forces, really has no excuse for its oddly executed campaign. Iran, on the other hand, has obvious and multitudinous excuses, deriving from a revolution which led to the disintegration of much of its military forces and abruptly severed the connections for maintenance, training, and supplies with its principal defense support. So, in the region's councils of rulers and officers' messes, it appears probable that assessments of Soviet doctrine, equipment and training will drop yet another notch. The very fact that Iran's F4s have been flying steady missions and that her F14s have apparently been used as radar stations for these F4s in some instances, suggests at least one transference of skills.

In Iraq, it is not yet clear how the course of the war will be viewed within Iraq's own military structure. At the moment, it would appear as plausible that discontent might enable the Soviets to rally Saddam Hussein's enemies to overthrow him, as that there might be a backlash against the Soviets as a scapegoat, particularly if they are perceived as aiding Iran. The fluidity of the Iraqi situation and its irony is at least equalled by Iran's predicament. Surely there will be pressures from within the surviving remnants of the Iranian military—and it appears that some units are very much together—to reconstitute at least some aspects of their U.S. supply relationship as logic gains a little over ideological fervor. However, the political costs of even a tentative resumption of U.S. supply appear as great for an Iranian leadership as for ourselves, at least until the war is settled and a clearer direction of leadership is evident in Teheran. But the lesson of Iraq's attack and its humiliation certainly implies strong pressures from all but the most extreme religious and far-left ideologues in Iran not to allow the same degree of military vulnerability to recur.

Here is the crux of the danger. Unless a very different kind of government emerges in Teheran, it seems unlikely that the armed forces will be trusted to the extent of reforming themselves in a major way, let alone reestablishing links with the U.S., no matter how attenuated. Should military pressure from Iraq continue, therefore, it would seem to open the way either for an argument to being a major military relationship with the Soviets or for one simply to rely on Soviet protection by developing close political ties. These are strong logical and historical reasons working against either of these courses, but logic has not been the hallmark of postimperial Iran. Nor would it be unprecedented to have the Soviets openly train and supply both sides of a combatant relationship, as we may recall from their activities in North and South Yemen.

Already surfacing, as a result of the war, are many queries on the subject of air defense. I refer not only to issues of why neither Iran nor Iraq seemed to have been able to utilize their elaborate systems to prevent deep penetration of their airspaces, but also to a heightened sense of vulnerability on the Arab side of the Gulf which is leading to substantial new requests for weapons systems. Inevitably, we will also see major new requests for larger stockpiles of ammunition and spares. The result, when coupled with existing requests from the Saudis, who have a newly credible rationale in their view, will be to place new strains on the crucial Saudi-U.S. relationship over the next five years. This strange war, fought so close by, and, for the first time in the region, I believe, without the presence of foreign advisors or technicians, will seem in Riyadh to have raised the level of probability of more conflict to come. The Iraqi shift of airborne forces down the Gulf to Oman in the early stages of the war in a (fortunately aborted) thrust for the Tunbs and Abu Musa islands, obviously brought home to the Saudis how close they came to air attack from Iran. Moreover, the Saudis observed that neither the Soviets nor the U.S. manipulated events in the war nor developed decisive leverage to bring it to a close. So a renewed impetus for the Saudis to leapfrog down the long road to military self-sufficiency is bound to generate pressures, only a portion of which may work to our ultimate advantage.

Those Saudis who focus on the purely military implications of this war will ask why there was no apparent air-ground coordination and such apparent looseness of command and control. Many in the military are fully aware that the increased ranges, speeds, and accuracies of weapons add sharply to the requirement for command and control improvement and for cohesiveness in the battle area. But the "ideal" version of this model would create unacceptable problems for a monarchy acutely conscious of the need for careful compartmentalization of forces. Will this add to internal Saudi political pressures?

Similarly, will not an increased Saudi military desire to have an orderly system that works run head on into the trend of very large increases in new weapons systems? Saudi forces, already straining unsuccessfully to meet the manpower demands created by agreements with the U.S. for naval and air modernization, are now confronted with substantial new commitments for major French naval and armor programs. This impacts on manpower shortages, a sore subject between different parts of the Saudi government, and works against efficiency in the sense of adding the burden of complex new logistics systems. And, as possible war looms more as a reality to the Saudi professional military, surely pressures will mount for more nonpolitical officer selections on merit, as opposed to traditional ways. As more and more highly sophisticated systems are acquired but yet not fully manned or absorbed, pressures will build for a greater foreign technician presence in the kingdom. The risks are obvious as an increasing proportion of the kingdom's manpower resources become committed to a process which is force fed and so dependent on foreigners as to seem to be a non-Saudi.

These dilemmas in the U.S.-Saudi relationship will be prominent in the eighties. For the U.S., the problem is not one of whether or not to continue major assistance for Saudi defense modernization, but rather how to help in a manner which creates the least amount of friction in Saudi internal affairs and in our own Congressional-executive branch relationships. The Saudi-U.S. relationship appears, in fact, to have been strengthened by the war and in response to upheavals in Teheran and Kabul. Moreover, there were slender threads of an informal Gulf alliance forming prior to the war and these now assume more body. Iran seems likely to be out of this alliance for years, as its search for internal stability overrides all else. Iraq, which may emerge from the war with a different ruler, but not a parliamentary democracy or a monarchy, will presumably become at least loosely a part of this alliance, as well as continuing to be a source of concern to the conservative Arab Gulf states. For this reason, strategic logic dictates that Egypt will reform its close ties with Riyadh so that an effective balance against Soviet subversion and Iran's turmoil can be achieved. The course of U.S. diplomacy concerning the West Bank, as well as the Palestinian population throughout the Middle East, and including Jerusalem and the Golan Heights, will be a key determinant in the viability of this reconciliation. American diplomacy which fails to discern the importance of Jordan's contribution to Gulf security will fall short. Equally essential will be an American ability clearly to distinguish actual Israeli security requirements from religious and political aspirations. The military factors which have brought Israel through a period of nonwar have not brought peace, and we now see the paradox of unparalleled Israeli military strength at a juncture where Israel's longer range national security in its full dimension is on the decline because of demographic, economic, and moral considerations.

For the eighties, then, we will come back again and again to the question of Palestine, no matter how remote its issues at first glance appear to be from the perspective of the Persian Gulf. The illusion that the two problem areas can be divided should finally have been put to rest by the current war, although some have asserted that we can now put West Bank autonomy and related issues on the back burner. Quite to the contrary, the regional lineup of support for either of the combatants relates to the essence of the Arab-Israeli problem. It is the moderates on that issue who confront the radicals, who place a higher priority on a solution to Palestine than on Arab solidarity. In all likelihood, a U.S. blunder on the basic Arab-Israeli problem would have more potential for unseating the Saudi monarchy than any capability the Soviets are likely to develop over the next five years to subvert the Saudi monarchy from within.

As the U.S. gears forward in building overall conventional capability and greater access to the Gulf area by means of access facilities and pre-positioned supplies, there will be a dangerous temptation, as we have noted, to push for the ultimate—full-fledged bases. The same temptation will exist as we see a fragile alliance among the Arab states of the Gulf assume cautious shape. In the latter instance, there will be those who, for the sake of good order, planning, and presumed deterrent power against the Soviets, will argue for a formal U.S. role in this alliance. Even the hastiest glance at history should discourage such an effort. The U.S. position in the area is uniquely wrapped in ambivalence, comprised of our role as Israel's benefactor, as possible predator in an oil-embargo crisis, as military supplier, and as possible protector. Such a composite does not make for an easy formal alliance.

Finally, the eighties will see recurrences of nostalgia in the military area that will have to be resisted. Several weeks ago, Joseph Harsch, a giant of the press, wrote a piece bemoaning the departure of British forces from the Gulf in 1971, noting that their presence cost only a few million annually. This he contrasted with the huge outlays now required to inch back toward any kind of equivalent capability. First of all, it is quite possible that we would today have several radical regimes on the Arab side of the Gulf had the British not withdrawn when they did: very large British forces could not sustain a British presence in Aden, which left under fire and whose legacy disrupts the area today. British or American forces in the numbers implied by Mr. Harsch would have done nothing to retain the Shah's position. Because it is not practical for the U.S. or the West to occupy the whole of the Middle East, we are far better off leaving colonial aspirations to the Soviets.